Judaism Straight Up

Why Real Religion Endures

מגיד

MAGGID

Moshe Koppel

Judaism Straight Up

Why Real Religion Endures

Maggid Books

Judaism Straight Up
Why Real Religion Endures

First Edition, 2020

Maggid Books
An imprint of Koren Publishers Jerusalem Ltd.

POB 8531, New Milford, CT 06776-8531, USA
& POB 4044, Jerusalem 9104001, Israel
www.maggidbooks.com

The publication of this book was made possible
through the generous support of *The Jewish Book Trust.*

ISBN 978-1-59264-557-2, *hardcover*

Printed and bound in the United States

Dedicated by Harold and Dolores Arnovitz
In honor of their children, grandchildren, and great grandchildren

Dedicated in awe and unending thanks to our parents,
Mr. and Mrs. Michael and Hilda Aaronson.
May we live by the values you embody
and pass them on to the next generation.

Contents

PART 4: WHERE ARE WE HEADED?

Preface

Most people I know live somewhat bifurcated lives. Their family and communal lives are characterized by strong ethnic and religious ties and traditional norms, while their lives outside family and community are saturated with contemporary Western culture, including its cosmopolitanism and its often dismissive attitude toward tradition. The subtle tango involved in reconciling these two worlds is as familiar to Buddhists and Hindus as it is to Christians, Muslims, and Jews.

I began this dance as a child in a Yiddish-speaking *ḥeder* (religious elementary school) on the Upper West Side of Manhattan and continue it today as a computer-science professor living in Israel. This book has grown out of my own efforts to integrate the seemingly disparate facets of my social, religious, and intellectual experience.

Many, if not most, people who live bifurcated lives don't feel that there is a problem to be solved. They simply speak two languages, using each as appropriate. Others believe that reconciliation is impossible. Some of them attempt to cut themselves off as much as possible from contemporary Western culture, building high walls around themselves and their communities in the hope, often vain, that the barbarians at the gates can be warded off. Others abandon traditional norms, or simply drift away from them, at least to the extent that family obligations permit.

This book is addressed mainly (but by no means exclusively) to those who have wrestled with the problem of maintaining deep traditional commitments while engaged with a cosmopolitan society that often denigrates such commitments. One of the reasons that such reconciliation is difficult is that even those who are deeply embedded in both cultures have a hard time putting their finger on the key underlying differences between their specific culture and the dominant Western one. Furthermore, certain norms and beliefs that are at odds with most religious traditions are so pervasive in contemporary Western society that one can hardly imagine them as anything but a part of the fabric of reality itself. They become the starting point from which traditional norms are judged – and, typically, found wanting.

In this book, I focus specifically on the particular tradition I know best: Judaism. Readers affiliated with other religious traditions can decide which of my insights carry over to their own experiences. I identify the most fundamental ways in which traditional Jewish norms and beliefs differ from those of the dominant culture, and in the process offer a somewhat novel primer on Judaism as it is actually experienced by some of its most devoted practitioners.

I have tried to frame the differences in a way that avoids the common pitfall of assuming the superiority – or, more precisely, the inevitability – of certain suppositions of contemporary Western culture. In particular, I endeavor to tease out the sacred beliefs and norms that render parts of progressive society something akin to a religious order of its own. It's my hope that once these beliefs and norms are made explicit and subjected to scrutiny, they'll lose the luster of inevitability.

The particular version of Judaism that I focus on is considerably more intuitive and experiential than the more text-based version familiar to most people who have received their religious education in institutions rather than in family or community settings. In fleshing out this organic version, I describe in considerable detail the views and attitudes of a particular character who personifies it.

The fact that I need to reach back two generations to find such a character is telling, and it might suggest that the version of Judaism I describe is a thing of the past. But I do not believe this is so. I have written this book precisely because I am convinced that the kind of organic Judaism I describe here can make a comeback of sorts, and I wish to make my own modest contribution to nudging it along.

One brief methodological comment is in order. Although I discuss political philosophy at some length, I have avoided the words *liberalism* and *conservatism*; although I use ideas taken straight from the theory of evolution, I hardly use the word *evolution*; although this is a book about religion, I skimp on using the word *God*. This is deliberate. Most people assume that the meanings of these terms (and many others I avoid) are well understood, when in fact they are loaded with ambiguities and hidden assumptions that require unpacking. I've tried, therefore, to simply spell out precisely what I mean rather than lazily hiding behind such terms. I hope that the benefit of speaking plainly outweighs the occasional jarring effect of an anticipated word's non-occurrence.

* * *

I owe thanks to many people. Thanks to Neal Kozodoy for encouragement, guidance, and advice from the beginning of the project. Thanks to Asher Meir, David Shatz, Abie Rabinowitz, Avi Shmidman, Russ Roberts, Elliott Malamet, and Yisrael Aumann, for numerous very fruitful conversations. Thanks to Hillel Gershuni for assisting with references; to Haviv Gur for helping make the book more fair to views I oppose; and to Ze'ev Maghen, whose encouragement reminded me how much this book owes to the wonderful essay he published in *Azure* twenty years ago.

I am grateful also to many people who read all or part of earlier drafts of the book and offered useful comments: Ed Aaronson, Elliott Abrams, Richard Aiken, Josh Amaru, David Arnovitz, Jeff Ballabon, Michael Berkowitz, Josh Berman, Yitzie Blau, Sarah Rindner Blum, Michael Broyde, Isaac Chavel, Eric Cohen, Shlomo Engelson, Stefanie Engelson, Elli Fischer, Netanel Fisher, Ralph Frankel, Azriel Ganz, Emmett Gilles, Heshy Ginsburg, Yehonatan Givati, David Goldman, Stefan Goltzberg, Mark Gottlieb, Eli Gurevitz, Danny Gutenmacher, Malka Rappaport Hovav, Seth Kaplan, David Kessler, Seth Avi Kadish, Jonathan Klahr, Yitzhak Klein, Arnold Kling, Steve Klitsner, Eugene Kontorovich, Roberta Kwall, Sam Lebens, David Leiser, Yechiel Leiter, Saul Lieberman, Elad Lison, Mishael Lobel, Jerome Marcus, David Matar, Yaniv Mezuman, Emmanuel Navon, Danny Orbach, Yehoshua Pfeffer, David Pilavin, Jay Pomrenze, Ido Rechnitz, Aryeh Roberts, Anat Roth, Chaim Saiman, Benjamin Schvarcz, Alon Shalev, Yitzchok Silber, Michael Weingrad, Joshua Weisberg, Aviva Winter, David Wurmser, and Jeff Zucker.

My thanks also to Matthew Miller and the staff of Maggid Books, especially editors Reuven Ziegler, Shira Finson, Caryn Meltz, Ilana Sobel, and Nechama Unterman, as well as art directors, Tani Bayer and Eliahu Misgav, with all of whom it has been a pleasure to work. I am grateful as well to Harold and Dolores Arnovitz and to the Aaronson family for their generosity in sponsoring the publication of this book.

Finally, this book is an expression of gratitude to my parents' generation of European refugees in the United States and an expression of hope for my children's generation of native Israelis. If not for the wisdom, kindness, and fortitude of my wife Channah, I would surely have been a wholly inadequate intermediary between them.

Introduction
Shimen and Heidi

It was in the kosher dining hall at Princeton where, in the early 1980s, I lost my innocence. In my first foray into life in a non-yeshiva environment, I was a newly minted PhD in mathematics with a one-year appointment to the Institute for Advanced Study. Heidi was a graduate student in the humanities who had taken it upon herself to educate me about the special duties of the Jewish people to humanity. "How can you justify your narrow tribal loyalty? Isn't the lesson of the Holocaust that we Jews must *never* put our parochial interests ahead of others' interests? We should know better than anyone what happens when that lesson isn't learned." That was the moment I realized that I had never encountered true orthodoxy before.

My own thoughts about Jewish obligation were somewhat less righteous than those of my interlocutor. My first lessons in the matter had been learned in the small *shtiebel* (prayer hall) on the Upper West Side of Manhattan where my grandfather prayed along with his fellow Gerer Hasidim.

Even several decades after The War, this *shtiebel* had the look and feel of the hundreds of its Gerer counterparts that dotted Poland before every one of them was destroyed in The War. They were focal points of Hasidism, a movement that, spreading through Eastern Europe in the nineteenth century, advocated a form of organization into tight-knit communities centered around a rebbe (spiritual leader), with an emphasis on the social and experiential aspects of Jewish observance accessible even to the less learned. The Gerers – named after the town of Gura-Kalwaria, where one of the rebbes lived for a time – were probably the largest and most learned of the hasidic sub-groups in Poland, its members numbering in the many tens of thousands, perhaps in the hundreds of thousands.[1]

The regulars at this particular *shtiebel* were among the few survivors of their families and communities. They retained their loyalty to the ways in which they had lived before The War, but without beards or the fur hats (known as *shtreimlekh*, or in the case of the taller version worn by Gerers, *spodeks*) typically worn by Hasidim on Shabbat and Holidays. They were God-fearing Jews, but they felt sufficiently at home with God to take liberties as necessary. They were worldly, cynical, and fiercely independent, but had chosen to remain loyal to the ways of their fathers. Although some were fully committed, others and maybe most might better be thought of as semi-lapsed Gerer Hasidim who nevertheless wouldn't think of jumping ship after what had happened to their families.

---

1. For some background in English on Hasidism in general and the Gerers in particular, see D. Biale et al., *Hasidism: A New History* (Princeton, NJ: Princeton University Press, 2018), a recent anthology on the history of Hasidism; and A. J. Heschel, *A Passion for Truth* (New York: Farrar, Straus and Giroux, 1973), on the Kotzker Rebbe, a forerunner of Gerer Hasidism, whose quirks provide insight into the Gerer mindset. Also of interest is H. Seidman, *Warsaw Ghetto Diaries* (New York: Targum Press, 1997), a Holocaust diary by a member of the band of Gerers that included Shimen and my grandfather.

My grandfather and Shimen, his best friend in the community, were of the latter variety. Shimen told many stories, all about the same topic. Here's an example: A Nazi officer in the Lodz ghetto demanded that he hand over either his son or his daughter within forty-eight hours. One of Shimen's profoundest sorrows, and he had many, was that his daughter sensed he had fleetingly thought to choose to keep his son. Up to the time both she and her brother were murdered, she never spoke to him again. After The War, Shimen got his hands on a pistol and went from house to house on a mission to extract Jewish children from the Polish families with whom they had been left when their parents were deported to the camps.

Elie Wiesel, who often prayed in that Gerer *shtiebel*, relates a story about Rosh HaShana, the Jewish New Year, in Auschwitz.[2] One of his fellow inmates announced to the rest of the assembled in the barracks that though they had no wine, "we'll take our tin cups and fill them with tears. And that is how we'll make our kiddush (a Holiday blessing made over wine) heard before God." That inmate was Shimen. Of course, Shimen had no patience for drama, and whenever the story was told he would scrunch up his eyes behind his thick black-framed glasses and say, dismissively, "Nu, Wiesel. He makes a living telling *maiselakh* (tales) about me."

The Gerer *shtiebel* gang were intense, they were angry, they could be funny in a biting sort of way, they were devoted. But one thing they had no patience for was high-minded pieties. They despised pomposity and self-righteousness. Their devotion to *Yiddishkeit*, old-fashioned Judaism, as a way of life, and to the Jews as a people, were as natural and instinctive as drawing breath.

For reasons not quite clear to me, to this day I see the world through their eyes. My instinctive judgments about most things are their judgments. My views are hopelessly, and proudly,

2. E. Wiesel, *One Generation After* (New York: Random House, 1970).

old-fashioned. In some odd way, I think of myself as an ex-Gerer Hasid without having ever actually been a Gerer Hasid.

The very cosmopolitan Heidi of Princeton, and the many, many Heidis I've met since then, patronize old Shimens as addle-brained relics out of touch with contemporary doctrines. First, Shimen's old-fashioned views evince what Heidi regards as an immoral preference for the welfare of Jews over that of others. Second, Shimen is committed to social norms that are mediated by rabbis and thus, in Heidi's view, insufficiently respectful of the autonomy of individuals. Third, Shimen's understanding of the world is rooted in a set of beliefs that are, to Heidi's understanding, ahistorical and unscientific.

In this book I'll present a defense of Shimen's cranky, old-fashioned view of the world – okay, my own cranky, old-fashioned view of the world – against Heidi's progressive pieties. My main argument will not focus on the misrepresentation of Judaism advanced by cosmopolitan critics like Heidi. Rather, I will argue on behalf of the provocative claim that Heidi's critique is rooted in her failure to fully grasp the nature and scope of morality, tradition, and belief necessary for *any* society to flourish.

In short, between Heidi of Princeton and Shimen of the Polish shtetl, one is narrow and orthodox and the other is worldly and realistic. I will argue in this book that most people are confused about which one is which.

* * *

The book will focus on three main differences between Heidi's world and Shimen's world.

The first difference concerns the scope of morality. Heidi is extremely sensitive to treating people unfairly or generally causing others distress. In fact, as far as she is concerned, this is the main moral litmus test; otherwise, no harm, no foul. By contrast, Shimen (of whom I'll speak in the present tense even though he is long gone) lives in a highly moralized world. What you eat, what you wear, and whom you sleep with are all fraught with moral considerations, whether or not anyone else is adversely affected. Furthermore, Shimen feels morally bound by particular loyalty to the Jewish people, deference to its scholars and elders, and reverence for institutions and objects sanctified by its traditions – again, even at the possible expense of others.

The second difference between Heidi and Shimen concerns the mechanisms through which communities determine and enforce the boundaries of the forbidden and the obligatory. For Heidi, though she is no great patriot, the relevant community consists of citizens of the state (or supranational entities); the best mechanism for determining obligations and prohibitions is public policy; and the method of enforcement is prosecution. For Shimen, who lives in the Jewish diaspora, the relevant community consists of those committed to the norms of the Jewish way of life, also known as halakha; the best mechanism for determining obligations and prohibitions is community tradition and practice, occasionally codified and augmented by expert opinion; and the method of enforcement is social pressure. In short, Shimen – though he is assuredly bound by laws, including the laws of the state – lives mostly in a world of social norms driven from the bottom up, while Heidi – though she is subject to plenty of social pressure – lives mostly in a world of laws driven from the top down.

The third difference concerns the relationship of one's beliefs about the world to one's social and moral commitments. For her part, Heidi aspires to ascertain the truth through the study of science and history and to base her commitments on such truths as best she can. For his part, Shimen's social and moral commitments precede his most important beliefs about the world – that is, his religious beliefs – and those beliefs are deeply intertwined with his moral commitments.

These three somewhat telegraphic claims will be discussed in detail in the following three sections of the book. In each, I'll begin with a primer on Shimen's world: respectively, the substance of halakha, the mechanisms through which halakha develops, and the nature and content of Jewish belief. This will be followed by a brief précis of Heidi's reservations about that world and an analysis of the differing assumptions and motivations that underlie the pair's divergent perspectives. Then I'll explain why every long-lived society that we know about is more like Shimen's than like Heidi's.

In the first section, I'll argue that societies need rich systems of social norms – including public rituals, food taboos, kinship rules, and commercial-exchange regulations – in order to cohere and survive. In the second section, I'll argue that, to remain viable, such systems of social norms must, like language, adapt to circumstances slowly and organically, and not, like legislated law, through sudden, theory-driven upheavals. Finally, in the third section, I'll argue that members of a society, in order to be willing to make the sacrifices necessary to sustain that society, must genuinely believe that they are part of a meaningful, directed project that will long outlive them.

In brief, I'll argue that Heidi's world is doomed.

* * *

Before we begin, a few words about what not to expect in this book.

Although I'll be discussing some classical Jewish sources, my arguments will not be drawn primarily from these sources. Rather, since my assumption is that my readers, whatever their religious sentiments, spend a fair amount of time, like me, in Heidi's world, I will be mostly arguing on Heidi's turf: classical and contemporary social-science literature, including anthropology and cultural evolution, moral psychology, game theory, and economic signaling theory.

Since morality is precisely the issue in dispute here, an argument against Heidi on grounds of morality itself risks being circular. So, to avoid even the impression of circularity, I won't be arguing that Heidi's world is morally deficient, but rather that it is simply not viable. To the extent that I do draw moral conclusions from this lack of viability, I'll avoid the naturalistic fallacy by being explicit about how they follow. Indeed, while the argument against Heidi's viability is itself, I believe, a damning one, this is not a how-to guide for any Heidi types who might be considering transitioning into Shimen types. If there's a roadmap for that, I don't have it.

By the same token, it's not my intention here to provide an exhaustive overview of all the types of characters and attitudes one finds in Jewish society. I chose Shimen and Heidi because they are good representatives of two common attitudes toward Jewish tradition – and tradition generally – that I wish to contrast, but I'm quite aware that most readers will probably not identify with either one of them.

I'm just as aware that my choice of Shimen and Heidi as the characters on which to hang my arguments has certain inherent limitations.

First, Shimen is a cranky old Polish Jew for whom many people might have sympathy, but he is certainly not a person with whom young readers can easily identify. By contrast, while Heidi (though she is by now middle-aged) is younger and more in tune with most contemporary readers than Shimen, portraying her as naive in comparison with someone possessing Shimen's life experience might strike readers as too easy an enterprise. At least in that respect, I haven't set up a perfectly fair fight.

Second, Shimen is a man in a society in which men dominate the public sphere; if I had chosen, for example, to compare Heidi with Shimen's wife, rather than with Shimen, this would be a very different book. It would likely be richer regarding the inner life – Gerer women are famously more open than Gerer men – but it also would be poorer regarding the public communal life that I wish to focus on. And, it must be said honestly, it would bring into sharp relief certain aspects of Shimen's world that, for better or worse, are less attractive to most contemporary readers than the ones I emphasize here.

Having said that, I will try throughout to represent Heidi's views fairly and to give her the strongest possible arguments on behalf of those views. If I can't contend with Heidi's best case, my argument will be weak indeed.

PART 1

What Is the Right Way to Live?

In this part of the book, we'll consider the most basic question of all: How should we live our lives? We'll look at the way Shimen lives his life and at Heidi's reasons for rejecting that way of life. In particular, we'll confront Heidi's main challenge to Shimen: What is the point of obligations and prohibitions that seem arbitrary and don't contribute to human flourishing in any apparent way? We'll argue that the kinds of norms to which Shimen is committed are necessary for a society's survival.

Chapter 1

Jewish Morality and Its Critics

After The War, Shimen did not return to the full hasidic dress that he wore before The War. There were aspects of hasidic life about which he became perhaps a bit less naively enthusiastic than he had once been. He was also quite angry – not at the perpetrators, whom he regarded as no worthier of his anger than rabid dogs, but mostly at those who failed to comprehend the enormity of what had happened or who espoused views that somehow blamed the victims. And, yes, he had a few bones to pick with the Creator, though for him this was an entirely intimate matter.

Nevertheless, for the most part, he lived his life in accordance with halakha, pretty much as he had before The War, and he did so in an extremely natural manner. While this naturalness might distinguish him from many contemporary practitioners of halakha, some of whom we will discuss below, the details of

Shimen's daily life as a Jew committed to halakha are hardly different from those of any halakhically observant Jew.[1]

I'll review these details now, mainly as a primer for those less familiar with halakha but also to reorient the reader already familiar with halakha from those aspects regarded by authorities as formally the most important to those aspects that are actually experienced most saliently in the everyday life of practitioners.

EVERYDAY SHIMEN

Immediately upon awaking on a typical weekday, Shimen will wash his hands in a ritual manner and recite the appropriate blessings. If he shaves at all, it will not be with a razor blade but rather with scissors or an electric shaver, and he will always leave ample hair on his temples. He will dress modestly and will wear a *tallit katan* (a garment with fringes called tzitzit) under his shirt and will keep his head covered at least partially at all times. He will not wear any clothing that includes mixtures of wool and linen. In public, he will usually wear a jacket and a hat, though not the long jacket (*bekeshe*) and round hat (*kapelush*) he wore before The War.

On most weekday mornings, Shimen will go to his *shtiebel*, don his full-size prayer shawl and phylacteries, and recite the morning prayers with a *minyan* (a quorum of ten men). He will treat religious articles with great reverence, pointing to the *mezuza* as he passes through a door frame and handling his phylacteries only in accordance with specified rules. He will stand for the Torah scroll when it is taken from or returned to the ark for the

---

1. As we shall see below, Shimen's routine reflects communal practices more than book knowledge. Nevertheless, the reader seeking more information about halakha might be well served by the literature, including: S. Ganzfried, *Kitzur Shulḥan Arukh* (Mesorah, 1864, trans. 2011), an English translation of an abridged (and stringent) code of Jewish law; H. Donin, *To Be a Jew* (New York: Basic Books, 1972), a summary of Jewish practice for the contemporary reader; C. Saiman, *Halakhah: The Rabbinic Idea of Law* (Princeton, NJ: Princeton University Press, 2018), a recent academic work on how rabbinic scholars have viewed halakha.

abridged readings on Monday and Thursday mornings, just as he would stand in the presence of a scholar of Torah.

During prayers, Shimen will put some coins in the charity box or in the hands of a beggar passing through. He will catch up on who in his community is ill or in mourning and will plan to visit them at the first opportunity. Although he is by no means a wealthy man, if a friend asks for a small loan, he will comply on the condition that no interest be paid; if he needs a small loan, he will expect the same conditions. When approached, Shimen will make a modest contribution to the maintenance of the *shtiebel*, the *mikve* (ritual bath), and other community institutions. All of Shimen's friends and acquaintances are Jewish, and almost all are from backgrounds very similar to his own.

Shimen's routine is broken for Shabbat and Holidays. For a twenty-five-hour period beginning on Friday evening just before sundown, he will observe prohibitions too numerous to list in full. For instance: he will not light or extinguish a fire or even turn a light on or off, not move money or make a transaction, not cook or even pour directly from a preheated kettle onto a tea bag, not write with a pen or a keyboard, not carry objects in an unenclosed space, not tie or untie any semi-permanent knot (like on a package), and generally not even speak of business and other mundane matters.

On Shabbat, Shimen will spend extra time in the *shtiebel* praying and listening to an extended reading of the Torah. After communal prayers on Friday night, he will recite kiddush at home over a cup of wine and then wash his hands and recite a blessing over two whole loaves of challah; this will be repeated in the morning after prayers; he will have challah again at the third Shabbat meal before sundown.

These Shabbat restrictions and rituals will be repeated with relatively minor variations on the Festivals, each of which has its own associated special rituals. Thus, Shimen will eat all meals during the seven-day fall Festival of Sukkot in an outdoor sukka (booth); during the spring Festival of Passover, he will neither eat nor maintain at home any foods, other than matza, that include grain; on the eve of Shavuot he will typically stay up all night studying Torah; and on Rosh HaShana he will spend extra time in the *shtiebel* and listen attentively to the blowing of the shofar. On Yom Kippur, he will fast for the entire twenty-five hours, spending most of it praying, focused on the theme of repentance.

On five other fast days during the course of the year, four of which commemorate events associated with the destruction of the First and Second Temples thousands of years ago, Shimen will fast from morning to night, except on Tisha B'Av, when he'll fast for a full twenty-five hours. On the minor festivals of Purim and Ḥanukka, he will commemorate miracles from the period of the Second Temple. On the eve of Purim and again in the morning he will go to the *shtiebel* to hear the reading of the Purim Megilla (scroll), and he will partake in a festive meal with friends in the afternoon. On Ḥanukka, he will light candles on the windowsill of his home for each of the eight days of the festival, adding one candle each night.

Shimen eats with considerable restrictions. He will buy meat only from a vendor under strict supervision, ensuring that the meat is from approved species, that the animal was slaughtered in a strictly specified manner, that certain parts of the animal were removed, and that the edible parts were soaked and salted appropriately to remove blood. He will not mix milk products with meat products or eat them at the same meal; in fact, he won't consume milk products for six hours after eating meat, and he won't use the same dishes or utensils for milk and meat. He will eat fish only from species with fins and scales. He will not eat any processed foods unless marked with a trustworthy seal of approval attesting that they contain no non-kosher ingredients. He will not eat agricultural produce of the Land of Israel without first ascertaining that symbolic tithes have been taken. He will drink wine only if it has been produced by Shabbat-observant Jews. He will not eat any food (fruit, vegetables, etc.) without first reciting the appropriate blessing for it, and will also recite appropriate blessings following eating.

Shimen will frequently attend life-cycle rituals – a *brit* (circumcision ceremony), a bar mitzva, a wedding – often addressing the assembled guests to share a thought based on the weekly Torah reading and his gratitude that Jews are once again capable of celebration. He will take pleasure in suggesting matches, *shiddukhim*, for his friends' children and grandchildren, the rules of which are well known to the participants: courtship is meant to be relatively brief, and the prospective mates are supposed to refrain from sexual activity, even touching. Engagement and marriage are regarded as creating a bond not just between two individuals but between two families, each of which undertakes financial obligations related to the well-choreographed celebrations surrounding the marriage and to the establishment of a new home. Even after marriage, couples are not permitted to engage in sexual activity while the wife is menstruating and for the subsequent week, after which she immerses in a *mikve*. They are expected, if they are able, to produce many children, with one son and one daughter regarded as a minimum. Abortion is forbidden, except in relatively rare circumstances. If the marriage fails, a *get* (writ of divorce) must be enacted in a very precise manner; a child born to a woman who has not obtained a valid divorce is regarded as a *mamzer* (illegitimate) and is almost unmarriageable.

Whenever he has free time, Shimen studies Torah; on any given day, he is working his way through one of the tractates of the Babylonian Talmud. The subject is only slightly more likely to be one of the matters enumerated above, most of which determine the texture of his daily routine, than matters that have been without any direct application to Jewish practice for the past two millennia.

For example, Shimen might study the laws of sacrifices brought in the Temple: categories of sacrifices, on what occasions they were brought, the sequence of the associated rituals, who was eligible to perform them, which errors of action or intention disqualified a sacrifice, and so on. He might study the laws of ritual defilement: the hierarchy of impurity from human corpses on down, the means by which contamination could be transferred to a person or object, the means of purifying a contaminated person or object, the proper handling of uncertainty regarding possible contamination, and so on. He would as soon study laws of torts and fines intended for application by specially ordained judges, not one of whom has existed for centuries, as he would the laws of ordinary debts and transactions that are still adjudicated on a daily basis.

Shimen works in the diamond business, interacting mostly with people with backgrounds like his own. In the rare event that some dispute needs to be adjudicated, he will – with the agreement of his counterpart – approach a local rabbinic scholar to propose a compromise or to rule in accordance with halakha. When Shimen needs to make an especially important personal decision about which he is uncertain, he might turn to the Gerer Rebbe for guidance.

This sketch merely touches the surface of halakha as it is expressed in daily practice, but it should give us adequate background to highlight some key distinctions from the very different moral principles preferred by Heidi, whose reservations about all of the above we can now consider.

HEIDI OF PRINCETON

Heidi's maternal grandfather studied in a yeshiva in Lithuania and came to the United States in the 1920s. He married a young woman from a fairly well-to-do American family and subsequently became the rabbi of a nominally Orthodox synagogue in a medium-sized city in the Midwest. His was the only Shabbat-observant family in the neighborhood. Heidi's mother and her two brothers went to public school; after school, her grandfather studied Talmud with the boys.

On her father's side, Heidi's grandparents moved to New York shortly after their marriage in Warsaw in the early 1930s. Jobs were hard to come by during the Depression; her grandfather worked in a kosher butcher shop, and her grandmother freelanced as a seamstress. There were few Jewish day schools available and, in any event, the family could ill afford one, so Heidi's father and his sister attended public school. They both went to the local Orthodox synagogue's Sunday School program.

Heidi's parents met in New York in the mid-1950s. Sharing a traditionalist sensibility that was already on the verge of becoming rare at that time, they married and moved to Long Island, where Heidi's dad worked as an engineer at a large firm and her mom worked as a schoolteacher. They became active in the local Conservative congregation, attending services often, if not regularly. Like her older brother, her only sibling, Heidi attended the local public school because it was regarded as excellent academically; almost all of her classmates and friends were Jewish.

Heidi attended after-school classes in the local synagogue; she could read Hebrew passably and was well versed in Jewish legends. She had good relationships with her Orthodox grandparents and even with her mother's brother's family, who had turned *yeshivish* (that is, strictly observant in a non-hasidic style) and lived in the Flatbush neighborhood of Brooklyn.

When she came to Princeton as an undergraduate in the mid-1970s, Heidi naturally gravitated to Stevenson Hall, the forerunner of today's Center for Jewish Life. Most of the students who dined at Stevenson came for the kosher food, but Heidi, whose family had observed the laws of *kashrut* only at home and not outside, simply felt comfortable in the company of other Jews. In fact, on Shabbat she sometimes attended egalitarian services, ones with mixed seating for males and females and with equal roles for women in leading prayers. After befriending Orthodox students who had returned from post-high-school programs at yeshivas in Israel, she also occasionally allowed herself to be pulled in to lectures on halakha.

When I met her at Stevenson Hall, Heidi was tall and graceful with a startling mop of curly black hair; she was attractive despite her almost complete lack of attention to her appearance. Blessed with a good sense of humor and an engaging personality, she was especially entertaining when riffing on her mother's Long Island Jewish accent and bourgeois manner. ("This house looks like a pig stoy! A *shanda* [embarrassment]! I have to clean it up before the girl comes" – the "girl," of course, being the house cleaner.)

Heidi's student days were for her a time of discovery, of expanding horizons, and of disappearing barriers. She wished to know all cultures, to love all people, to drink the world in whole. And she made friends easily. By her junior year, her social circle, including Black, Hispanic, Muslim, and Hindu friends, began to resemble the General Assembly of the United Nations.

At first, this only reinforced her fondness for Judaism. Even if her friends didn't quite get most of her jokes, witnessing their evident ethnic pride increased her appreciation of her own ethnic identity. Gradually, though, she felt her ethnic loyalties under challenge, in two ways.

First, she became keenly aware of the utter arbitrariness of her own particular identity. Second, she became sensitive to the financial, social, and cultural obstacles that many of her new friends had to overcome in order to be accepted to Princeton and survive there, and she began to feel guilty about her own advantages as a white and relatively wealthy American.

From this new point of view – it might be called the view from nowhere, and it certainly accorded no privilege to Judaism – she began to reassess her Jewish attachments. Her Orthodox friends and relatives seemed a bit, well, provincial. Their professed beliefs seemed so random as to be either insincere or the product of brainwashing. Their concern with picayune details of halakha also seemed somewhat obsessive, and it apparently sapped them of energy for the truly important social-justice causes crying out for attention.

But most of all, halakha itself, as practiced by her Orthodox friends, struck her as suffering from serious moral failings. In particular, it appeared to encourage in its practitioners a certain hostility to non-Jews. She had always known that Jews were opposed to intermarriage; for reasons becoming increasingly vague to her, her parents had mentioned their own abhorrence of the idea on several occasions. But at Princeton she had discovered that Jewish disdain for non-Jews extended well beyond that.

She once attended a lecture by the local representative of Chabad – a hasidic sect that, unlike the Gerers, engages in outreach – on the topic of Jews and non-Jews. Despite his effort to present an idyllic picture, it slipped out in the question period that observant Jews do not collect interest for a loan to a fellow Jew but are allowed to take interest from a non-Jew. In the chaos that ensued after she protested this injustice, it further emerged that observant Jews don't drink wine handled by non-Jews. She never attended another class on Judaism.

As Heidi distanced herself gradually from the small Orthodox scene at Princeton, she became more sensitive to what she perceived as a certain condescension not only toward non-Jews but also toward non-observant Jews like herself. She noticed that when discussing Torah, her more religiously observant acquaintances would switch into a private language she felt was deliberately intended to exclude the uninitiated.

But in the final analysis, what really turned Heidi off to Judaism was its attitude toward women. On the rare occasions when she attended the Orthodox congregation for an event she couldn't avoid, she would quietly seethe behind the *meḥitza* (partition) that separates men and women in such congregations. She recalled her mother's unspoken resentment at not having been included when her own father had studied Torah with her brothers. When attending a traditional Jewish wedding, Heidi understood the ceremony well enough to reach the conclusion that Jewish marriage was a patriarchal institution, entered into by the man's "acquiring" a wife. She took to referring to Judaism as being "oddly essentialist" in regarding men as inherently different from women, and Jews as inherently different from non-Jews.

In brief, the Judaism for which she once had a certain atavistic fondness now seemed unnecessarily restrictive, confining, and narrow. It squelched universal love in the name of obscure, particularist principle. By the time I met her, Heidi was far more committed to what she regarded as social justice than to any form of Judaism, and she came to the kosher dining hall mostly to educate innocents like me on the immorality of our version of Judaism.

Was there merit to her claims?

Chapter 2

Moral Foundations: Fairness, Loyalty, Restraint

Shimen and Heidi do not, to put it mildly, see eye-to-eye on the right way to live. In this chapter, we'll get to the heart of their disagreement.

The anthropologist Richard Shweder interviewed six hundred subjects in a variety of communities in India and the United States about their moral beliefs.[1] He summarizes his findings with the observation that there are three distinct categories of moral principles that one finds, in varying proportions, across human societies – and three concomitant types of violations of these principles. Let's call these categories fairness, loyalty, and restraint.

---

1. R. A. Shweder, N. C. Much, M. Mahapatra, and L. Park, "The 'Big Three' of Morality (Autonomy, Community, Divinity) and the 'Big Three' Explanations of Suffering," in *Morality and Health*, ed. A. M. Brandt and P. Rozin (Florence, KY: Taylor & Francis/ Routledge, 1997), 119–69.

Fairness involves respect for others' freedom and rights; violations of fairness are characterized by harming someone's person, dignity, or property, or by not caring for them adequately. Loyalty involves respecting and honoring one's community and its institutions; violations are characterized by derelictions of familial, communal, or national obligations. Finally, restraint involves respect for the natural order; violations are characterized by impurity, decadence, and degradation.

Shweder's student, the social psychologist Jonathan Haidt, elicited the opinions of many thousands of people all over the world regarding a set of moral dilemmas based loosely on the earlier Shweder interviews.[2] He presented the dilemmas in the form of stories involving such activities as stealing a desperately needed drug, consensual incest, eating the family pet, mopping the floor with the national flag, and so forth.

Haidt's key conclusion is roughly this: There are two kinds of people in the world. Members of more traditional communities tend to assign approximately equal importance to all three moral categories, which he calls "foundations." But educated Westerners with progressive political views differ. They tend to assign great importance to the first foundation, fairness, and very limited importance to the other two, loyalty and restraint. (Strictly speaking, Haidt subdivides Shweder's three foundations into either five or six foundations, but this doesn't change the main contours of the story.)

How well does this difference between traditionalists and progressives explain the differences between the attitudes of Heidi and Shimen toward Jewish tradition? As a first approximation, pretty well.

---

2. Jesse Graham, Brian A. Nosek, Jonathan Haidt, Ravi Iyer, Spassena Koleva, Peter H. Ditto, "Mapping the Moral Domain," *Journal of Personality and Social Psychology* 101, no. 2 (2011): 366–85.

The halakhic life places great emphasis on all three moral foundations – to repeat: fairness, loyalty, and restraint. In fact, the three moral foundations correspond to three types of biblical commandments familiar to most Jews from the question of the wise son in the Passover Haggada (based on Deuteronomy 6:20): "What mean these testimonies (*eidot*) and decrees (*ḥukkim*) and rules (*mishpatim*)?"

The commandments referred to here as "rules" are those that order society by regulating the duties of each individual to other individuals; these correspond to fairness. In the Torah, they are commonly subdivided into *tzedek* (righteousness) and *ḥesed* (benevolence). These include, for example, the duty to be honest in business and to give charity to the poor.

The commandments called "testimonies" are those that manifest the Jewish duty to bear witness to God's dominion on earth by according special respect to the people, objects, and institutions that most saliently represent that duty; these correspond to loyalty. In the Torah, they are commonly subdivided into *kavod* (respect) and *yira* (reverence). These include, for example, the duties of honoring parents and teachers, of participating in communal prayer, and of observing Shabbat and the Festivals.

Finally, "decrees" are commandments that seem arbitrary but signal subservience to God's rules; these correspond to restraint. In the Torah, they are commonly subdivided into *kedusha* (sanctity) and *tahara* (purity). These include, for example, the duty to restrain our gustatory and sexual appetites in particular ways and the prohibition on wearing blends of wool and linen.

For simplicity, I'll refer to violations of fairness, loyalty, and restraint, respectively, as harm, disrespect, and degradation. Not coincidentally, the three major sins that the rabbis of the Talmud say must be avoided even at the cost of one's life – murder, idolatry, and incest – are simply the extreme cases of these three types of violations.[3]

* * *

For Heidi, on the other hand, the fairness foundation is far more important than the others. Her objections to halakha all involve the special loyalty of Jews to each other reflected in halakha and the constraints that halakha places on human choice. Haidt's general distinction, between traditionalists who roughly equally value all three moral foundations and progressives who value fairness more than the other two, explains the differences between Shimen and Heidi quite nicely.

But let's not overstate the case. Shimen is deeply suspicious of non-Jews and is not eager to have much to do with them, but he is a resolutely decent human being. Without giving the matter much thought, Shimen gives considerable weight to fairness.

Shimen might have proposed reciting kiddush on tears in Auschwitz, but it wouldn't cross his mind to do it on a stolen bottle of kosher wine in Manhattan. He knows that under certain circumstances one can violate a prohibition in order to observe a positive commandment (like wearing ritual fringes made of a prohibited weave of wool and linen),[4] but again it would never occur to him that this principle would extend to violating one's duties to other people (a principle so commonsensical that it has never been disputed and was not even made explicit by any rabbinic commentator prior to the nineteenth century).[5] Shimen knows the difference between being *frum* (pious) and being a *mensch*.

---

3. Sanhedrin 74a.
4. Menaḥot 40a; Yevamot 4a.
5. The point was first made by Rabbi Moshe Sofer in *Ḥatam Sofer* on Sukka 42a, who writes that the alternative is "unthinkable."

Shimen, like most Gerer Hasidim, doesn't linger long over the reading of the *haftara*, the brief section from the Prophets chanted on Shabbat after the Torah reading, but he perfectly understands the verses in the *haftara* read on the Shabbat preceding the fast of Tisha B'Av: "For what do I need your many animal sacrifices? God says. I have enough burnt offerings.... Stop doing evil, learn to do good. Seek justice, defend the oppressed, do justice for the orphan, argue for the widow."[6]

Shimen might not recall an observation in the Talmud[7] concerning a verse from Isaiah, "The righteous, if good, eat the fruits of their deeds" (3:10). The observation goes: "Can there be righteous people who are not good? Rather, one who is righteous to God and good to people will eat the fruits of his deeds." To which the fourteenth-century sage Rabbi Asher ben Yeḥiel adds: "For God prefers deeds that also do good for people over those only between a person and his Creator."[8]

Even so, Shimen understands all this. So he does take the fairness foundation very seriously – at least as long as it doesn't conflict with his uncompromising allegiance to his fellow Jews.

And Heidi, to do her justice, does not put *all* of her moral eggs in the fairness basket. She shares Shimen's revulsion at disrespect and degradation. She shares his instinctive sense that incest, for example, is wrong. She agrees that speaking ill of one's deceased father, even if nobody is harmed by such speech, is wrong. She is as revolted by cannibalism as any traditionalist, even if the deceased has died naturally and willed his body for this purpose. Nor does she have any intention of gathering the family around the table to dine on their recently deceased Chihuahua.

---

6. Isaiah 1:11–17.
7. Kiddushin 40a.
8. Commentary to Mishna Pe'ah 1:1.

So Heidi is not completely insensitive to the loyalty and restraint foundations.

What this means is that the differences between Heidi and Shimen are limited – for the simple reason that senses of fairness, loyalty, and restraint, even if somewhat inchoate, are part and parcel of human nature, and neither Heidi nor Shimen can escape them.[9] By contrast, matters of detail and emphasis are culture dependent, and on these matters Heidi's culture and Shimen's culture diverge widely. In Heidi's culture, fairness is given much greater importance than loyalty and restraint.

This is manifest in two ways.

The first becomes evident when, as Jonathan Haidt did, you present people with potted stories involving completely private and unreported acts of cannibalism or incest and ask not just *if* this is bad (almost everyone instinctively agrees that it is), but rather *why* it's bad.[10]

With regard to incest, for example, traditionalists like Shimen might say that the Torah forbids it or that it's wrong and degrading, and that its wrongness requires no further explanation. Progressives like Heidi, on the other hand, would struggle to find some way in which someone would be harmed: offended sensibilities, deformed babies, regrets, irreparable relationships. In Heidi's culture, causing harm or being unfair to others is a primary violation, while violations involving disrespect for community hierarchy, disloyalty to the tribe, degradation, or dissoluteness are at most secondary. Such violations are either wrong, because they can be somehow interpreted as causing harm, or else they are regarded as mere violations of social convention. ("That's not

---

9. For a pioneering and spirited defense of this point, see J. Q. Wilson, *The Moral Sense* (New York: Free Press, 1993). Wilson speaks of four moral foundations, rather than Shweder's three or Haidt's five or six.

10. Jonathan Haidt, *The Righteous Mind: Why Good People Are Divided by Politics and Religion* (New York: Pantheon Books, 2012).

what we do around here but, so long as no one is harmed, what others do is their business.")

This leads directly to a second way in which fairness is privileged in Heidi's culture. When two different moral foundations rub up against each other, fairness always wins. Thus, if particular consensual sexual interactions are regarded as dissolute, as they were in Heidi's family culture until recently, but restrictions on such interactions can be seen as oppressive to those with non-standard preferences, the outcome is now clear. The very idea of dissoluteness now sounds archaic to Heidi. Similarly, if Jews marrying non-Jews was regarded as a betrayal of tribal loyalty in Heidi's family culture until recently, but restrictions on intermarriage can be seen as intolerant, the resolution is now obvious. The very idea of tribal loyalty now sounds bizarre to Heidi.

By contrast, for all that Shimen's piety is accompanied by sympathy, taboos remain taboos. Restraint and loyalty are, for Shimen, self-justifying moral foundations. And if the norms that manifest them in his culture sometimes cause harm to some individuals, this is unfortunate but necessary.

Shimen may not feel any need to justify the restraint and loyalty foundations, but we do. Let's now turn our attention to that project.

Chapter 3

The Need for Social Norms

In this chapter, we'll make several main points. First, social norms manifesting all three moral foundations are central to societies in all times and places. Second, the reason for this is that many of these norms are necessary in easily understood ways for holding a society together. Third, even those norms that do not have any obvious rationale have subtle and important utility for social solidarity.

A methodological note: Much of what I'll be writing here draws upon raging debates about the evolution of morality. My views are consistent with those who hold that moral instincts in individuals are genetic adaptations sometimes detectable even in non-human primates;[1] that social norms are products of interactions between cultural evolution and genetic evolution;[2] that

---

1. Frans de Waal, *Primates and Philosophers: How Morality Evolved* (Princeton, NJ: Princeton University Press, 2006).
2. Joseph Henrich, *The Secret of Our Success: How Culture Is Driving Human Evolution, Domesticating Our Species, and Making Us Smarter* (Princeton, NJ: Princeton University Press, 2016).

natural selection can act at the level of the group and not just at the level of the individual;[3] and that religion often represents a kind of group adaptation.[4]

Nevertheless, I won't explicitly discuss the controversies surrounding these claims; for the most part, the differences among the antagonists are considerably less momentous than the intensity of the debates would suggest. More importantly, I won't assume the reductionist underpinnings of many of the arguments on all sides of these debates – specifically, that morality is "nothing but" a set of evolved preferences or utility-maximizing rules. To assert, as I do, that viable moral systems must be adaptive and must increase certain kinds of collective utility is not to reduce morality to these properties.[5]

CERTAIN TYPES OF SOCIAL NORMS ARE UNIVERSAL

For many East African peoples, eating fish is taboo. In India, widows do not eat fish. In Fiji, pregnant women don't eat fish. Jews eat only those fish that possess both fins and scales.

For Yazidis, lettuce is taboo. Chinese Buddhists don't eat garlic. Jains refrain from eating onions. Mormons abstain from coffee and tea. Some North American tribes, mostly around Berkeley and Cambridge, will not eat food that has traveled great distances. I personally will not eat *p'tcha* (jellied calves' feet, a dish favored by Eastern European Jews of a certain age), for all the money in the world.

---

3. David Sloan Wilson and Elliott Sober, "Reintroducing Group Selection to the Human Behavioral Sciences," *Behavioral and Brain Sciences* 17, no. 4 (1994): 585–654. The Wilson and Sober article is followed by responses.

4. S. Atran and A. Norenzayan, "Religion's Evolutionary Landscape: Counterintuition, Commitment, Compassion, Communion," *Behavioral and Brain Sciences* 27, no. 6 (2004): 713–30. The Atran and Norenzayan article is followed by responses.

5. James D. Hunter and Paul Nedelisky, *Science and the Good: The Tragic Quest for the Foundations of Morality* (New Haven, CT: Yale University Press, 2018).

Muslims often marry first cousins. Catholics and North Indian Hindus regard that as incest. South Indian Hindus and some tribes in Fiji allow marriage between cross-cousins (children of a brother and a sister) but not parallel cousins (children of two brothers or of two sisters). For Jews and Protestants, marrying a first cousin is allowed, but nowadays it's regarded as weird. In twenty-nine American states, marriage between first cousins is illegal.

In some places and industries, deals are sealed with the signing of a contract, in others with a handshake. Sometimes the transaction isn't complete until delivery is taken. Two Gujaratis in the once Jewish-dominated diamond business close a deal by saying "*mazal ubrakha*" (Hebrew for good fortune and blessing).

Just about every society has rules about who holds the door open for whom, when to shake hands or bow, how far apart to stand during a conversation, how to determine status and how to address someone of a given status, how to inquire about someone's welfare and how not to respond, when it's okay to brandish a weapon, and who gets to lead the rain dance.

For all the astonishing variety of social norms one finds in the wild, one can't help being even more astonished by the ubiquity of certain *types* of norms. Consider this brief description, by the anthropologist Joseph Henrich, of the four types found in the bush: "kinship ties, social norms of ownership, food taboos, and ritual practices."[6] Sounds sensible, right? It would also ring a big bell with students of Jewish law who noticed the correspondence of this description with the material covered in the four sections of the *Shulḥan Arukh* (the sixteenth-century code of Jewish law compiled by Rabbi Yosef Karo): *Even HaEzer* on marriage; *Ḥoshen Mishpat* on monetary matters; *Yoreh De'ah* on food prohibitions; and *Oraḥ Ḥayim* on rituals.

---

6. Henrich, *The Secret of Our Success*, 165.

It seems these types of norms are simply universal, though (as we saw above) the specific norms themselves vary widely. Let's consider the four types in a bit more detail (now using not Henrich but the standard order of the *Shulḥan Arukh* and other Jewish codes):

- Ritual practices: These include communal prayer and observance of lifecycle events and periodic Festivals. All are governed by rules defining the roles accorded to various members of the tribal hierarchy in such practices.
- Food taboos: These constrain the types and combinations of foods that may be consumed, prescribe the means of preparing foods, and define the requirements of sharing different types of foods.
- Kinship ties: These are governed by rules regarding which marriage relationships are permitted, who pays whom and what when a marriage is contracted, how the family unit is defined, the duties of each spouse, the degree of fidelity expected from each partner, and the rules of succession for inheritance.
- Social norms of ownership: These concern the rights and duties of ownership, the means of completing transactions, the definition and consequences of various torts, and the disposition of public goods.

It is straightforwardly plain that these types of norms formalize each of the moral foundations we considered earlier: sharing and other forms of fair play, duties to community, and constraints on animal pleasures.

Why so many rules? Why not just "no fighting, no biting"? Granted, our intuitive moral sense is usually too vague for practical purposes, and it competes with all sorts of selfish inclinations that further muddy the waters. It's good to have clear rules that settle the matter without much mental or emotional energy being required. Still, why do all societies have so *many* rules?

Apparently, no society would survive for long without them.

SHARED NORMS MAKE SOCIETIES VIABLE

One evening in 1941, a boatload of European refugees, including my father's family, anchored on the shores of Casablanca, Morocco. The boat's passengers were herded into a refugee camp; the only way out, they were told, would be for local families to come and take responsibility for them – presumably only a theoretical possibility, since the passengers were unlikely to have any acquaintances there willing to take them home. By morning, the local Jewish community had caught wind of the situation; not a single Jewish family remained in the camp.

It was indeed the beginning of some beautiful friendships. But what's the secret to this kind of solidarity? One part of the answer, the part that concerns us now, is shared norms.

Solidarity, trust, and cooperation make up the stuff now often called *social capital*. Without it, a society wouldn't last long. The creation of social capital among members of a society is possible only if shared norms align their expectations, habituate them to exercise self-control, instill in them a unity of purpose, and incentivize them to transmit wisdom across generations.

In short, social norms must encourage our prosocial instincts and discourage our selfish instincts. If you and I both know that we share a commitment to such norms, we can trust each other and cooperate in mutually advantageous ways.

Let's see how the norms considered above – rituals, food taboos, kinship rules, and exchange regulations – achieve these ends. For best effect, as we go through this, think of hunter-gatherers rather than religiously observant Jews.

Consider the public performance of such rituals as prayer, singing and dancing, rites of passage, ostracisms, coronations, exorcisms, communal ingestion of psychotropic substances, and whatnot. Each such performance is carried out according to established rules governing who does what, where, and when. Individuals sharing particularly powerful experiences often feel an overwhelming sense of unity, belonging, and common purpose, almost a kind of melding into a single organism. (If you have a hard time imagining communal prayer doing the trick, think about communal ingestion of psychotropic substances.)

Furthermore, younger participants in public rituals see that elders and wise people are accorded honor, and understand implicitly whom they should take as role models. In this way, they learn to value experience and knowledge, and they understand that if they wish to obtain similar prestige, they should seek to acquire such experience and knowledge. They also internalize the tribe's division of ritualized responsibility and develop the qualities of character appropriate for best performing their respective roles. In addition, privately performed rituals, such as minor blessings or meditative activities, encourage mindfulness and introspection and, under special circumstances, can evoke a sense of awe and unity.

Food taboos, as well as rules of purity and contamination, serve the incidental purpose of reducing possibilities for eating or contacting toxins. Along with other constraints on consumption – ritualized slaughter of animals, blessings over food, feast-related ceremonies, sacrifices – they help cultivate the ability to defer pleasure and draw attention to the differences between humans and animals.[7] Rules regarding tithing and other obligatory food gifts build solidarity and trust and promote the internalization of a sense of mutual responsibility.

---

7. Leon Kass, *The Hungry Soul: Eating and the Perfecting of Our Nature* (Chicago: University of Chicago Press, 1999).

Next, norms regarding kin relations. Prohibitions on polyandry and rules regarding female fidelity in marriage reduce paternal uncertainty and thus encourage paternal responsibility. Limitations on polygamy prevent violence among males competing for scarce women.[8] Institutionalized assortative mating, such as, among Jews, the matching of promising male scholars with wealthy brides, incentivizes scholarship and improves the gene pool.

It is well understood that prohibitions on incest prevent defects associated with inbreeding, but actually they achieve much more. The fact that incest is not merely prohibited but is a flagrant taboo engenders intra-family trust by completely eliminating sexual tension within the family unit; this permits unthreatening intimacy among family members. Analogously, when homosexual acts are taboo, male cohorts – hunters, soldiers, yeshiva students – can interact with complete trust and even intimacy uncolored by sexual tension.

As for exchange regulations, voluntary trades are beneficial for both sides of the transaction; a multitude of such transactions thus greatly benefits the entire society. But such commerce is possible only if buyers and sellers share an understanding of the rules of the game – when a transaction is complete, when and where delivery will take place, who is on the hook for defects, etc. – and can trust each other to carry out their respective parts of the deal. Norms of commerce manage expectations, create the necessary degree of trust, and reduce transaction costs to everybody's benefit.

To summarize: All of the types of social norms we have considered here promote trust and cooperation, sometimes in subtle and indirect ways. This is why they are so crucial to a society's flourishing.

---

8. Joseph Henrich, Robert Boyd, and Peter J. Richerson, "The Puzzle of Monogamous Marriage," *Philosophical Transactions of the Royal Society* B 367, issue 1589 (2012).

SOME BIZARRE NORMS HAVE SIGNALING VALUE

It's all well and good to talk in the abstract about the social capital that accrues from rules and rituals, but how well do such claims hold up when we consider concrete examples?

Take, for example, the hasidic custom of wearing a *shtreimel* (fur hat) on Shabbat and Holidays and at family celebrations. Shimen and most of his Gerer friends abandoned these hats for reasons I'll discuss below, but the greater mystery is why they and their ancestors – and some of their descendants – ever adopted the custom in the first place. To be clear, I'm interested here not in the particular historical circumstances under which this specific custom was adopted, but rather in what social benefits, intended or unintended, are promoted by such customs.

As any casual observer could hardly fail to note, a *shtreimel* is expensive, it isn't very comfortable in the summer, and it might attract unwanted attention on West End Avenue. All in all, it seems to be a rather costly quirk without much obvious payoff of the sort we discussed above.

In fact, however, viewed in a broader anthropological context, a *shtreimel* in summer is a walk in the park. Some Shiite Muslims observe the holiday of Ashura by whipping themselves with blades on chains; some Australian aboriginal boys pass a bone through their urethras to mark their passage into manhood, perhaps a bit too literally; participants in the Phuket Vegetarian Festival drive spikes through their cheeks and other soft tissue (don't ask what goes on at the Carnivore Festival); and bored youths all over the world cover their bodies in irremovable tattoos and pierce sensitive body parts.

What's this all about?

It's actually pretty simple. Consider my dear friend, Free Rider, a bit of a loser with poor financial prospects and no particular religious convictions. While wandering aimlessly through Boro Park, a hasidic stronghold in Brooklyn, Free chances upon a wedding, and, lo and behold, it looks like open house for the after-dinner potato kugel. Free soon discovers that there's a wedding in that particular congregation about five nights a week, there's an after-prayer snackfest on Shabbat, everybody is generous with charity, and there are volunteer societies devoted to giving free loans, visiting the sick, matchmaking, and so forth.

Free vaguely intuits that this system can work only if, on average, all in the congregation give as much as they get. But he figures he's just one person; even if he contributes nothing, which is precisely his intention, how much kugel can he eat? Nobody will notice or care.

Unfortunately for the optimistic Mr. Rider, however, many others have thought similar thoughts, and this particular congregation, as well as every other society on earth, would have long ago gone out of business had it been without means of smoking out Free Rider and his ilk. Every society requires that members, or wannabe members, signal they're serious about giving as much as they get and not just eating the kugel and running.

The trick of an effective signal for this purpose is that it must be worth sending only if you're a reliable type, committed for the long haul. If anybody, even Free Rider, can send the signal, it would be worthless.

Consider some roughly analogous situations. If you've opened a bank and want to signal potential depositors that you're not running off to Brazil with their money next week, build a big marble building, since that kind of investment is worthwhile only if you intend to be in business for a long time. If you want to signal employers that you're a productive worker, get a college degree;[9] you might not learn anything relevant to the job (or anything useful at all), but you presumably couldn't have gotten the

---

9. A. M. Spence, "Job Market Signaling," *Quarterly Journal of Economics* 87, no. 3 (1973): 355–74.

degree without a modicum of intelligence and diligence. If you want to signal to your fellow gang members that you're not planning to grow up and go all middle-class on them, tattoo SATAN on your forehead. If you're a peacock and want to convince the peahens that you have what it takes, strut enough useless plumage to exhaust a lesser man.[10]

Note that these signals work in different ways. The peacock's plume simply can't be mimicked by the unqualified. A college degree can be obtained by someone not especially bright or diligent, but it might require so much effort that it wouldn't justify the investment. Tattoos work by burning bridges out of the gang, very much the way that, in Israel, not getting an education and not serving in the military burn bridges out of certain communities.

What all of these signals have in common, though, is that they are costly. If they were cheap, Free Rider would mimic them. That *shtreimel* is persuasive only because it's expensive, hot, and marks you as an outsider in modern society. You would have to consume a whole lot of free kugel before you could recoup that investment, not to mention the cost of getting circumcised, learning Yinglish, and possibly even having to eat *p'tcha*.

It's worth adding that, while these signals serve as barriers to entry for outsiders like Free Rider, they also work for veteran members of a community, who signal their ongoing commitment to each other, thus maintaining the group's social capital. Signaling not only reflects commitment, but reinforces it; when I receive signals, my trust in the community is strengthened, and when I send a signal, my investment in the community is increased. Groups that demand adherence to certain kinds of social norms are better adapted than other groups and are more likely to survive and proliferate. Indeed, we shouldn't be surprised that a study

10. Amotz Zahavi, "Mate Selection – a Selection for a Handicap," *Journal of Theoretical Biology* 53, no. 1 (1975): 205–14.

of nineteenth-century communes by the anthropologist Richard Sosis found that the longevity of a commune was positively correlated with the number of demands it made of members.[11]

Finally, while many apparently bizarre social norms serve as signals that enable us to distinguish people we can trust from free riders, it does not follow that this is the (sole) purpose of such norms or the reason we should observe them. Peacocks don't strut their plumes because they *choose* to signal their strength and virility; rather, the instinctive urge to strut plumes serves as such a signal and thus has certain advantages for fertility. Similarly, those who observe rituals need not – and generally do not – do so for utilitarian reasons, even when the command to observe such rituals is accompanied by promises of timely rain and other worldly rewards. But the purity of practitioners' intentions aside, those who are faithful to communal rituals do in fact reap the rewards of communal solidarity.

REPEATED GAMES AND MORAL FOUNDATIONS

A society is not viable without cooperation among its members. We have argued that such cooperation requires adherence to social norms that reflect all three moral foundations: fairness, loyalty, and restraint. As that is the central point of this chapter, we can make it more forceful by considering a formal model of human interaction that abstracts away everything but the bare-bones issues.

What follows might be somewhat heavy going, but it is worth the investment.

Imagine two spies, Gadi and Palti, working in tandem, who have been captured and placed in separate interrogation cells. They are each offered the same deal: If you rat out your buddy

11. R. Sosis and E. R. Bressler, "Cooperation and Commune Longevity: A Test of the Costly Signaling Theory of Religion," *Cross-Cultural Research* 37, no. 2 (2003): 211–39.

and he remains silent, you'll go free and he'll go to jail for life and never be seen again (but just bear in mind that your friend got the same offer). If you both rat, you'll both get long prison sentences (though not life sentences); if you both remain silent, you'll both get short prison sentences.

At first blush, the last condition suggests to each of them that remaining silent is the way to go, and certainly better for both of them than if they both rat. But, thinking it through more carefully, Gadi realizes that, while he doesn't know if Palti will rat or be silent, he, Gadi, is better off ratting either way: if Palti rats, Gadi had better rat, too, or he'll never be seen again; if Palti is silent, Gadi need only rat to be free as a bird.

This reasoning is absolutely compelling; in fact, it's so compelling that Palti comes to the same conclusion. Thus, the two of them will have many years in a cell together to discuss whether ratting was the right choice.

We don't need to be prisoners to face the Prisoner's Dilemma, as this exercise is commonly called.[12] The essential elements are (a) that two parties can either honor (possibly implicit) agreements with each other – in the case of the Prisoner's Dilemma, an agreement to remain silent – or cheat; (b) that the parties must make their choices independently and simultaneously; and (c) that the ordering of preferences from *my* point of view is:

<I cheat, you honor>	is better than
<both honor>	is better than
<both cheat>	is better than
<I honor, you cheat>.	

---

12. The Prisoner's Dilemma is covered in any game-theory textbook. For a popular presentation, see William Poundstone, *Prisoner's Dilemma: John Von Neumann, Game Theory and the Puzzle of the Bomb* (New York: Doubleday, 1992).

This comes up in many real-world situations. A buyer and a seller can benefit from a transaction, but each can profit more by cheating at the other's expense. Two world powers can benefit from an agreement to avoid an arms race, but each can profit more by cheating. In all of these cases, a rational player would cheat.

One can extend this reasoning to situations with more than two players. For example, if we all do light fishing in a communal lake, we'll all have lunch and a lake full of fish; if we all do heavy fishing in the lake, the fish will be depleted faster than they can reproduce and we'll all have lunch and supper but a dead lake. So, I figure to myself, one possibility is that enough others will fish heavily to deplete the lake anyway, so I might as well live it up while I can. The other possibility is that enough others will restrain themselves, so I can afford to live it up, because the chances are negligible that my few extra flounders will tip the scales. The only hitch is that if everybody else thinks the same thing we can kiss the lake goodbye.[13]

How do we get out of this dilemma? It's obvious that we *can* get out of it because merchants, for example, do make deals all the time without cheating each other.

One possibility is that we are simply altruistic. We each have, as I have been arguing all along, an instinctive moral sense. So, I might not rat out my comrade for the simple reason that his well-being and freedom are important to me. This is quite true – but, alas, a careful analysis of human behavior suggests that while altruism is common, it is far from an adequate explanation of observed human cooperation.

A more plausible explanation can easily be intuited by contemplating our friends Buyer and Seller. It is true that Buyer can make extra profit by taking delivery and then not paying, and Seller can make extra profit by shipping counterfeit merchandise. But

---

13. G. Hardin, "The Tragedy of the Commons," *Science* 162, issue 3859 (1968): 1243–48.

how many times can they get away with this before others refuse to do business with them? Buyers and sellers who want to stay in business for the long term care about their reputations; in fact, online marketplaces make this explicit by enabling participants in a transaction to rate the other side. The Prisoner's Dilemma, a one-shot event, is thus not a fair representation of actual human interactions, which typically are ongoing and repeated.

To try to capture human interactions with a slightly more realistic model, let's consider the case of repeated Prisoner's Dilemmas: We play one round, the players' choices are revealed, and payouts are made; then we play the next round, and the next, and so on. Each player wants to maximize his payoff over time. What can we say about the behaviors of rational players in this scenario? Are they doomed to cheat as in the one-shot version? Note that whereas in the one-shot version a player needs to choose between two options (honor or cheat), in the repeated version a player needs to choose from among many possible strategies: always honor; always cheat; alternate between cheating and honoring; cheat if the other player cheated in the previous round but otherwise honor; and so forth.

Unlike the one-shot Prisoner's Dilemma, there is no single strategy that offers a maximal payoff independent of the other player's behavior. If the players are limited to strategies that are blind to the other player's past actions, then always cheating is indeed the best strategy. But a player can do better by being *responsive* to the other player's past actions.

Consider, for example, a strategy called "tit-for-tat," in which a player cheats only if the other player cheated in the previous round; in other words, he honors in the first round and then mimics the other player forever after. If Buyer is using this strategy, then under most circumstances Seller will maximize his own payoff by playing the same strategy (and the same is true from Buyer's perspective). In this sense, the situation in which both players use this strategy is an *equilibrium*, a concept we'll encounter several times as we go along. While this equilibrium is not the only possible one for the repeated Prisoner's Dilemma, it is a particularly happy one in that both players cooperate forever.[14]

Did you notice the "under most circumstances" that I slipped into the previous paragraph? Let's get back to that. Assuming Buyer is playing tit-for-tat, under what circumstances will it actually be optimal for Seller to honor the agreement as long as Buyer honors it as well?

The answer is that it depends on how much Seller values future returns. Suppose Buyer and Seller make a transaction exactly once a day. Assuming no one cheats, each gets one unit of joy from the deal. If they keep this up for a year, they'll each eventually earn 365 units of joy.

But how much is the unit of joy that Seller is expecting to get a year from now worth to him *today*? Presumably less than one full unit: if Seller is a live-for-today kind of guy, it's worth a lot less than a full unit; if he's a save-for-tomorrow kind of guy, only a little less. In the first case, we say that Seller has a high discount rate – that is, he greatly undervalues future returns relative to immediate returns; in the second case, we say he has a low discount rate – that is, he regards future returns as only slightly less valuable to him than immediate returns.

Here's the punchline: if and only if Seller has a high discount rate, it might be worth it for him to cheat. It's easy to see why: he'd rather make a quick buck at Buyer's expense today than make more than that in the future, since he heavily discounts the

---

14. The full range of possible outcomes for the repeated Prisoner's Dilemma is captured by "the folk theorem," so called because it was well known to game theorists before it was formally proved. For a formal presentation, see R. J. Aumann and L. S. Shapley, "Long-Term Competition – A Game-Theoretic Analysis," in *Essays in Game Theory*, ed. N. Megiddo (New York: Springer, 1994). More generally, see R. Axelrod, *The Evolution of Cooperation* (New York: Basic Books, 1984).

future. A guy with a high discount rate is a guy you don't want to do business with.

So, for long-term cooperation, we need players with low discount rates who choose a tit-for-tat strategy. But, as the legal scholar Eric Posner notes,[15] there's one more requirement. Let's call people with discount rates low enough for them to honor their agreement the *good types;* the guys with the high discount rates are the *bad types.* It's not enough for Seller to be a good type; he also needs to convince Buyer that he's a good type so that Buyer will want to do business with him.

In the formal model, is there actually a way for Seller to persuade Buyer that he's a good type and will deliver the goods? Posner's answer is yes. Let's think about those 365 units of joy Buyer and Seller might each get if they do business together. If Seller is a bad type, those 364 future units of joy are worth, say, 50 units of joy today; if he's a good type, they might be worth 250 units of joy today. So, if and only if Seller is a good type can he afford to give Buyer a gift worth 100 units today in anticipation of getting it back through future business. The gift signals to Buyer that Seller is a good type.

In real life, there are numerous ways that people signal that they're good types. They dress and groom themselves in ways that suggest they can afford to pay a price in money, time, and effort in order to profit from long-term cooperation. They are polite, as formal as necessary, careful about table manners, and generally make a display of their ability to control impulses. Of course, they do this not only in interactions with specific business associates but in interaction with their whole society.

Different communities develop different sets of behaviors for this purpose. By demonstrating a willingness to sacrifice for the community's well-being, and deference to its authorities and

---

15. Eric Posner, *Laws and Social Norms* (Cambridge, MA: Harvard University Press, 2002).

customs, members of a community convince others that they are good types who can be depended on to cooperate for the long term.

Now let's sum up. The requirements for cooperation in a community are tied to *all* three moral foundations we considered above: a preference for fairness (tit-for-tat), the ability to defer pleasure (low discount rates), and loyalty to the community and its institutions (signaling trustworthiness). And this, then, is the reason that all traditional communities share social norms that manifest all three moral foundations: fairness, restraint, and loyalty. They couldn't survive without them.

Moving on, we'll next see what happens when a society values the fairness foundation much more than it values the other two moral foundations.

Chapter 4

The Perils of Fairness Alone

Fairness, deferral of pleasure, and expressions of group solidarity are all necessary for cooperation. This can, however, be tricky, since the three foundations are sometimes in tension with each other. If my close compatriot is involved in an altercation with an outsider, loyalty and fairness might pull me in opposite directions. Furthermore, it is plain that requiring deferral of pleasure and conformity to social norms exacts a higher price from some people than for others; some people have idiosyncratic preferences. A sense of fairness inclines us to be solicitous of such preferences, while social norms regarding restraint and loyalty often pull in the opposite direction: such norms only work, in the ways we described earlier, if the kind of norm violations associated with idiosyncratic preferences are met with public disapproval.

In the face of this tension, Shimen's version of Judaism has settled upon a somewhat delicate balance between fairness, on the one hand, and restraint and loyalty, on the other – often favoring the latter. But, as I discovered in the encounter with which I began this book, Heidi pulls strongly in the direction of fairness. Perhaps this shouldn't surprise us. Restraint and loyalty are, at least at first blush, a lot more valuable for a community like Shimen's, which has struggled to survive in the face of persecution and limited resources, than for a secure and prosperous community like Heidi's, which can afford to be open and expansive.

But, as we will now see, the crucial question isn't in which direction one pulls, but rather whether a stable balance has been achieved. In the absence of such a balance, a pull toward one extreme can quickly morph into a slide to the opposite extreme.

HEIDI CAN'T SUSTAIN A SOCIETY

A year after our conversation, Heidi finished up her Master's degree at Princeton, decided to forgo the PhD program, and headed off for a few months of backpacking through Europe. She passed through Israel and was both charmed by its egalitarian spirit and dismayed at its provincialism and militarism. At her parents' request, she dutifully visited a great-aunt and -uncle, nodding politely as they burdened her with their experiences in The War, and shrugging off their clumsy attempts to set her up with a "fine young man." A week after arriving in Israel, she was relieved to cross the border into Egypt.

Once back in the United States, Heidi rented a small apartment on the Upper West Side of New York City and found a job working at a small non-profit organization that sent medical personnel and supplies to West Africa for the treatment of the symptoms of long-term cyanide poisoning. The hours were long and consisted mostly of administrative chores, but she enjoyed the warm glow of saving lives – and she took full advantage of the weekends. She had her Saturday rituals: first, jog around the reservoir in Central Park, then stock up on deli supplies and bagels at Zabar's, and finally browse for books at Shakespeare and Company – lingering in the critical studies section, but buying fiction by Grace Paley or Alice Munro. If she wasn't out too late partying, she'd buy the Sunday *Times* on Saturday night and luxuriate over the crossword puzzle on Sunday morning.

Heidi enjoyed the pace of life in Manhattan and generally visited her parents, who had retired to Boca Raton, only for Thanksgiving, Passover Seder, and Yom Kippur. One year she stayed in Manhattan for Yom Kippur and, on a whim, went to services at a local Reform temple. But she found it church-like and unfamiliar, and was perplexed by the religious significance that the congregants seemed to attach to "breaking the fast."

Heidi was already well into her thirties when she fell in love with a French journalist, Serge, who had come to interview her about her work at the non-profit. After living together for almost five years, Heidi and Serge got married in a civil ceremony and moved to New Jersey. Heidi couldn't bear the thought of her husband performing Catholic rituals in their home, so they agreed that they would live a life free of all religious encumbrances.

These days, Heidi does occasionally experience an atavistic pull toward folk tradition. Nevertheless, she always resists it, not because of the deal she made with Serge, to whom she is no longer married, but because Jewish ethnic and religious solidarity and the constraints they impose are ideologically troublesome for her. She believes that even the apparently voluntary performance of rituals is actually the result of subtle familial and social pressure that must be resisted. She's doubly opposed to a society using institutional power to promote any specific conception of virtue, even if only among those who have chosen to be part of that society. So long as someone's behavior doesn't directly and visibly affect anyone else, Heidi is convinced that this isn't her business and it shouldn't be any of your business. Insofar as this conviction is manifest in resistance to state coercion, for example, it is laudable, as we will see in Part 2. But to the extent that it means that a society ought not demand of its members any moral standards that extend beyond fairness, it is unlikely to work out the way Heidi anticipates.

A commitment to fairness alone can never be sufficient. Without a strong commitment to the other moral foundations – restraint and loyalty – fairness cannot be sustained. As we saw in the discussion of the repeated Prisoner's Dilemma in the previous chapter, fairness requires that we value the future almost as much as we value the present; those who live for today are not reliable long-term partners. Similarly, fairness is most likely to thrive in a society that values particular virtues not tightly tied to fairness – qualities of character like courage, temperance, prudence, and gratitude – which are best cultivated by a rich system of social norms.[1]

Fairness alone, as practiced and advocated by Heidi, often proves to be a rather delicate, even self-undermining, creature for a number of additional reasons: it requires a degree of detachment rarely achieved, it can encourage bad behavior in others, and it undercuts love. Let's see why.

Heidi values fairness above group loyalty. And, as far as she's concerned, the Jews are the group to which she must not be loyal. Neutrality can be elusive that way. Although she genuinely aspires to fairness, Heidi's inability to be indifferent about the Jews undermines that fairness. If Heidi were to chance upon the Republic of Freedonia, a democratic country in a bad neighborhood that had policies identical to those of the State of Israel, she might very well have nothing but admiration for the citizens of that plucky little country; she certainly wouldn't be writing letters to the *New York Times* denouncing them. If some New Jersey township were hunting for ways to keep American Vulcans with

---

1. Jonathan Sacks, *The Great Partnership: Science, Religion, and the Search for Meaning* (New York: Schocken, 2011).

pointy ears and quaint traditions from flooding into their neighborhood and acting altogether like Vulcans, Heidi would be leading demonstrations against the troglodytes. But when American Hasidim with curly earlocks and quaint traditions wish to move into her neighborhood, she's more likely to be found on the other side of the barricades.

It happens, though, that even some versions of authentic fairness can be problematic. For example, Heidi wishes to help those she perceives as lagging behind, especially if they belong to some disadvantaged group, by putting a thumb on the scale for their benefit. This sentiment is admirable. But the overly enthusiastic pursuit of equality is liable to result in greater inequality. Enthusiasts are drawn to simple solutions, and the simplest method for quickly diminishing inequality is to punish winners and reward losers. And, Heidi's protestations notwithstanding, not every group that fails is virtuous and not every group that succeeds is exploitative. Support for the underdog is often support for the least cooperative and most aggressive and dysfunctional actors, who leverage the moral and economic largesse showered upon them to wreak havoc upon their neighbors. Apart from undermining the very fairness Heidi wishes to advance, associating failure with virtue and rewarding it is a sure recipe for encouraging it. Rewarding failure drives a race to the bottom in which it is more profitable, at least in the short term, for some people to parade real or imagined victimhood than actually to make an effort to succeed.

Finally, love isn't fair. Care for others is typically rooted in a spirit of generosity that is first learned within the family. The circle of those with whom we interact with special generosity can be gradually expanded, but necessarily remains anchored in kinship and shared norms. Think of a person's generosity as a sand pile: The pile is highest at the center and tapers off as the distance from the center grows larger, just as our generosity will always be greatest for those closest to us and will taper as connections become more remote. The amount of available sand – our time, energy, and resources – is limited, so there is only so much one can flatten the pile before nothing is left of it. To love everybody equally is to love nobody.[2]

*   *   *

Apart from the fragility of pure fairness, a society that lacks a rich enough system of shared norms rooted in all three moral foundations is unlikely to develop the social capital required to sustain its own flourishing over the long term.

Heidi and her friends share similar academic and professional backgrounds and, especially, political views. But these similarities are mostly defined by what they are not. Heidi's crowd is not held together by kinship or ethnicity, by a shared history, or by a rich system of social norms. It is held together to a large extent by the disdain with which it regards the norms that it rejects.

Shimen, on the other hand, does share a rich system of social norms with his compatriots. As a result, he can walk into a Gerer *shtiebel* anywhere in the world and find people who remember his family, who share friends and acquaintances with him, who speak his dialect, who know what he knows, who understand what he needs, who exchange just the right kinds of stories and jokes with him, who invite him into their homes as a matter of course, and who do business with him on the basis of a handshake and a nod. Heidi can walk into a progressive conclave and find people who share with her a passion for fair-trade coffee and a fear of Republicans.

I exaggerate, of course, but limited social capital is only part of the problem. Many of the preferences revealed by Heidi's life

---

2. This point is made with great force in Ze'ev Maghen, *John Lennon and the Jews: A Philosophical Rampage* (Jerusalem: Toby Press, 2015).

choices suggest that she discounts the future considerably more than, for example, her concern about climate change lets on.

Like almost all of her friends, Heidi chose not to marry until she was close to forty, and chose to have only one child. She regards the family structure that sustained most human societies for millennia as an option no more valid than any other; her admirable compassion for those for whom traditional family life is unsatisfying blinds her to the devastating long-term consequences of low birthrates and the breakdown of the family.

In some ways, what is seen and immediate is more important to Heidi than what is unseen and long-term. Heidi is a pacifist. She doesn't identify sufficiently with any country to wish to make sacrifices in its defense; she discounts alarm about palpable threats to societies of which she is a member as paranoia and warmongering. In the short term, to be sure, her society can withstand military threats based on residual deterrence and the efforts of others, but in the long term, her society will lack the grit and spirit of self-sacrifice required to withstand the barbarians when they reach the gates. Similarly, Heidi favors economic policies that mitigate inequality in the very short term but distort incentives in ways that, as a vast economic literature indicates, will slow economic growth that could alleviate poverty in the long term. Finally, Heidi's subversion of traditional norms regarding the inception and end of life reduces the incidence of unwanted children and the misery of debilitating terminal illness – undoubtedly worthy goals – but a lackadaisical attitude toward abortion and euthanasia could ultimately cheapen life and sabotage our resolve to preserve and protect it.

Most importantly, this kind of discounting of the future does not remain stable; it leads to a cycle of decline. Heidi's high discount rate diminishes her society's prospects, and the dimness of these prospects further raise Heidi's discount rate; her society's prospects could thus be in permanent decline. More concretely, as social historian Mary Eberstadt argues,[3] those who, like Heidi, are not committed to a religious tradition will on average have fewer children, and those who have few children are less likely to commit to a religious tradition; birth rates among Heidi's cohort are thus likely to continue to decline. Similarly, those who don't identify with a tight-knit community inevitably undervalue the moral foundations, loyalty and restraint, that require a community, an attitude that further alienates them from any such community; these indispensable moral foundations are thus liable to continue to lose appeal.

Tragically, while Heidi's society declines, it isn't the relatively wealthy and educated like Heidi who are the first to bear the brunt of the decay. It's the poor and uneducated who suffer the most from the disintegration of families and religious communities, who have the dimmest prospects in a slow-growing economy, and who fight the wars that Heidi and her friends won't.[4]

HEIDI AND AMBER

Heidi, then, enjoys a wide circle of like-minded friends, but her world is short on tight-knit communities that generate social capital, commitment to having children, and willingness to make sacrifices to defend against threats to its security. One might therefore imagine, as suggested above, that the main threat to this world is that it would slowly peter out. But in fact it might be eaten by its own children.

Shortly after she and Serge married, and a year before they split up, Heidi gave birth to their daughter, Amber. Amber is now a student at Oberlin, majoring in colonial and environmental studies. She rarely acknowledges her Jewish roots other than to

---

3. Mary Eberstadt, *How the West Really Lost God* (West Conshohocken, PA: Templeton Press, 2013).

4. Charles Murray, *Coming Apart* (New York: Crown Forum, 2012).

occasionally begin remarks hostile to Judaism or to Israel with the words "As a Jew..."

Amber doesn't share with Heidi the memory of a real community, of a large and committed family, and of grandparents who could speak of genuine persecution. Amber needs something to give her life direction, and the standard tribal membership that was enjoyed by her grandparents, and that served her mother as a silent anchor, isn't going to work for her. So she has enlisted as a foot soldier in the struggle for social justice.

Like many of her fellow student progressives, Amber doesn't share her mother's rather benign notions of fairness. Heidi believes that harmless activities engaged in by people in the privacy of their own homes are nobody's business. For Amber, this is entirely inadequate. Amber believes, for example, that everyone has a positive moral obligation to affirm the virtue of sexual activity that Heidi once regarded as taboo, and that a failure to do so under certain circumstances should be prosecutable. Amber also believes not only that euthanasia and abortion should be legal but that they are positive rights and that doctors should be obligated to perform them on demand.

It turns out that once Heidi's "live and let live" principle is deemed passé by the likes of Amber, the door is open to a broad regime of morally charged dos and don'ts. Heidi's rather vague aspiration to fashion a new moral world out of what she imagines to be rational considerations opens the door to Amber's moral world – an ersatz religion that makes traditional religion seem benign by comparison.

Let's consider some of the Commandments in Amber's religion.

First, whatever sexual taboos Amber has overcome have been sublimated into a bewildering array of food taboos. Amber won't eat produce unless it's organic, locally grown, not genetically modified, and processed by union labor. She's vegan and avoids trans fats, nightshades, and any dish that suggests cultural appropriation. If keeping kosher is a way of life, keeping Amber's diet is a crusade.[5] Following Heidi, Amber's concern for the long-term future is focused not on the advancement or preservation of civilization but rather on the preservation of the natural environment. Her concern for the environment, which she regards as threatened by the encroachment of civilization, is fraught with religious symbolism. For Amber, recycling is a system of rituals and shrines (many of which are actually harmful to the environment),[6] and she regards those who question orthodox views on global warming as deniers or heretics, better condemned or shunned than reasoned with. Her dismissal out of hand of certain potential solutions to global warming, such as nuclear power or sulfur dioxide pumping, suggests a bias against any approach that doesn't serve the higher purpose of curtailing the spiritual contamination of the world by technological advance.

The point is more serious than Amber's hypocrisy or lack of self-awareness. Developed religions like Judaism serve to subdue the instinct for idolatry and primitive religion, the kind that encourages superstition, self-debasement, seclusion of untouchables, and human sacrifice. The process that we are witnessing as we move from Heidi to Amber sometimes looks like primitive religion reasserting itself in the absence of developed religion.

Judaism facilitates expiation of sin through relatively harmless means – in ancient times, through animal sacrifice (admittedly, not harmless to the animals), and today, through prayer

5. See Mary Eberstadt, "Is Food the New Sex?" *Hoover Institution Policy Review*, February/March 2009.
6. John Tierney, "Recycling Is Garbage," *New York Times Magazine*, June 30, 2006; Mike Munger, "For Most Things, Recycling Harms the Environment," *American Institute for Economic Research*, August 14, 2019, https://www.aier.org/article/for-most-things-recycling-harms-the-environment/.

and repentance. Other religions have their own methods, some more harmless than others. But, when Communist regimes, for example, suppressed developed religion, they reinvented aspects of primitive religion, including ritualized public confession of sins and self-flagellation, re-education in proper doctrine, and, for those who failed the final exam, human sacrifice on a grand scale.

Amber isn't quite there yet, and hopefully she's not headed in that direction, but the same untamed religious instincts appear to be at work. For Amber, the sin of contaminating Mother Earth with her carbon footprint can be expiated with symbolic offsets, but the sin of white privilege requires – and indeed is being increasingly met by – grueling public confessions. Holdouts can be publicly shamed and shunned and sent for diversity and sensitivity training. Perhaps this too can be regarded as a form of sacrifice.

In short, Heidi's soft cosmopolitanism could very well not simply peter out slowly but rather be replaced by a radicalized version of itself that undercuts the very freedom that is meant to be at its core. Like some overly enthusiastic *baalei teshuva* (lapsed or disconnected Jews who then returned to traditional practice), Amber's unacknowledged religious tendencies lack the nuance of more experienced and worldly-wise people like Shimen, who are committed to time-tested traditions.

In fact, Shimen and the rest of the Gerer survivors have quite well-developed senses of humor, especially about religion. They aren't nearly as earnest as the oppressed Amber of Oberlin. But I suppose they can afford it. After all, as Amber might solemnly instruct you, they've lived the privileged lives of cisgender white men.

THE ROOTS OF JUDEOPHOBIA

We have seen, then, that too much freedom can lead to a revolt against freedom. We'll now see that it's also the case that an exclusive emphasis on a single moral foundation, fairness, can lead to a revolt against fairness.

If Heidi is self-conscious about her Judaism and tries a bit too hard to demonstrate her neutrality, Amber lives in a Manichean political universe in which individuals are irrevocably assigned either to the Sons of Light or to the Sons of Darkness according to gender, sexual orientation, race, religion, nationality, and so on. There are, of course, disagreements about relative status in the pecking order within the ranks of favored sexual identities or disfavored nationalities, etc. But whatever the fine details of your preferred victimhood hierarchy, one thing must remain sacred if you wish to remain a member in good standing in Amber's world: you must hate Israel too.

If we hadn't grown accustomed by now to this bizarre state of affairs, it would strike us as deeply disconcerting. Why does Amber, a champion of sexual ambiguity in all of its permutations, have a soft spot for gay-lynching Muslim regimes while accusing gay-friendly Israel of "pink-washing"? Why does Amber, a self-professed champion of the weak and downtrodden, identify with a league of large Islamic nation-states that wish to destroy one small Jewish nation-state?

We can begin to entertain the mystery of Amber's own Judeophobia only in the context of a broader question: Why have so many different people despised the Jews for so long? In the Middle Ages, religious Christians reviled Jews for rejecting Christianity; in the nineteenth century, secularized Christians reviled Jews for engendering Christianity. When racism was acceptable the Jews were despised as an inferior race, and when racism became disreputable the Jews were despised for being racist. During the heyday of nation-states, the Jews were hated for persisting as minorities in other nations' states, and in the incipient post-nation-state era, Jews are hated for having their own nation-state.[7]

---

7. For an exhaustive history of Judeophobia, see R. Wistrich, *A Lethal Obsession* (New York: Random House, 2010).

I think there's a more parsimonious explanation for why Jews have been so reviled. In a word, they are messiah-killers. But not *that* messiah.

Think about the vibe the world gets from Shimen – and from Israel. It goes something like this: We Jews have our own ways. We eat differently, dress differently, pray differently. We're a tribe with our own hierarchies, and we look out for each other. In short, we have our own moral system, including restraints and loyalties. We hold you in contempt for murdering us or, in the best case, remaining indifferent to our murder, but we're prepared to live and let live. We won't treat you like family, but we'll be fair if you'll be fair. And we'll live this way for a good long time until the true Jewish Messiah arrives.

There are two implied claims here. First, that we can live according to our own distinct moral rules and nevertheless be fair with others; particularist traditions can be reconciled with fairness to outsiders. Second, that while a messianic era will come one day, we must wait for it patiently. These claims are so deeply ingrained in Judaism that outsiders suspect, often correctly, that anyone raised in a Jewish community, even Heidi, has at least partially internalized the message. And many of them hate the Jews for it.

Why? Most of the world has been and continues to be committed to one or another version of monochromatic utopianism: different groups, each in its own way, wish to bring salvation now by choosing either particularism or universalism to the exclusion of the other. They are exasperated by Jewish patience in waiting for an ever-deferred Messiah, and they are incensed by the Jews' implicit insistence on the possibility of reconciling particularist traditions and loyalties with fairness to others.

Almost nobody can abide these Jewish claims. Not those Christians who wish to bring salvation now through universal acceptance of Christ. Not those Muslims who wish to bring salvation now through the restoration of the Caliphate. Not racists who wish to bring salvation now by eliminating inferior races. Not enlightened philosophers who wish to bring salvation now through the triumph of reason over religion. Not post-nationalists who wish to bring salvation now through world government. Not Ambers who wish to bring salvation now through liberation from the responsibility of growing up and maintaining civilization.

They all despise Shimen – and, by association, even those mostly disaffiliated Jews, like Heidi, who are rather befuddled by this – for stubbornly rejecting their chosen path to salvation. The religious and racial supremacists hate Shimen for clinging to his own traditions and loyalties – and for demonstrating that it is possible to do so while being a decent person. For the enlightened ones, who insist that fairness can be achieved only by abandoning particularist commitments, the opposite holds: they can abide, or at least patronize, Muslim supremacists precisely because the latter don't presume to be fair. Muslim supremacists are playing to win and they say so. So, even as they reject Amber's belief in the importance of fairness, such supremacists implicitly uphold a more fundamental contention underpinning her worldview: that fairness and particularism cannot be pursued simultaneously. But Jews like Shimen reject the very foundation of the enlightened worldview: they presume to be fair even while maintaining their own traditions and loyalties. To the enlightened ones, this is an unforgivable heresy.

The impatient can't maintain their footing for long on the narrow path that runs between the abyss of fire-breathing particularism and the abyss of starry-eyed universalism. And when they slip off, as they must, they can't resist pulling at the coattails of the Shimens who stick stubbornly to the path – the path that turns and winds and slowly ascends.

* * *

The key takeaway of Part 1 is that social norms can serve both primary and secondary purposes. They can advance cooperation directly or they can merely develop qualities of character and serve as signals that facilitate trust. Societies, like Shimen's, that maintain social norms that serve all these purposes can thrive; societies that see value only in those norms that advance cooperation directly and transparently cannot.

The arguments presented here are somewhat preliminary, but they suggest that exploration of the mechanisms through which different norms advance these various ends in different societies could serve as an organizing principle for a fruitful research program.

We should not imagine, though, that we could ever be clever enough to use our reason alone to conjure such a system of social norms on our own. Rather, we must allow such systems to develop gradually. This is the topic of Part 2.

PART 2

How Do We Decide What Is Right and What Is Wrong?

In Part 1, we considered the *substance* of right and wrong and the differences between Shimen and Heidi regarding that issue. In this part, we'll discuss the *mechanisms* for resolving what is right and what is wrong. We'll confront Heidi's argument that Shimen's community lacks both the expertise to formulate optimal norms and the institutions required to legislate and enforce any norms at all. The questions we'll deal with include: How can norms be maintained and adapted in the absence of legislation and enforcement? What is the best type of community for making collective moral decisions? To what extent should such decisions rely on existing traditions? What is the appropriate balance between moral intuition and reason?

Chapter 5

Jewish Traditionalism and Its Critics

What does an observant Jew like Shimen learn about halakha from books and what does he learn from actual practice? When does he decide on his own what needs to be done and when does he consult authorities? When does he follow his instincts and when does he use reason? How does he reconcile his religious commitments and his political commitments? I'll first address these issues as they appear to Shimen and only then try to explain what is going on under the surface.

HOW SHIMEN DECIDES WHAT'S RIGHT

Shimen is committed to the traditions of his family and community. If he ever checks the written codes of Jewish law or consults with rabbinic authorities regarding some course of action, he does so only to ascertain the tradition as it is practiced in his community, not to amend it or bypass it. For Shimen, the "community" is a set of concentric circles beginning with his (dead) family, extending to Gerer Hasidim, and extending further to others committed to the Jewish way of life; the farther out the circle, the less weight it earns in Shimen's calculus.

Since every actual set of circumstances is unique, it is often hard to pinpoint a well-defined course of action prescribed by tradition. Each delicate social situation, each complicated financial transaction, each inadvertent mixture of permitted and forbidden foods, each ad hoc action on Shabbat, requires a judgment, often on the spur of the moment. In situations that call mainly for common sense and decency, Shimen's first instinct is to conjure up what his *bubbe* (grandma) would do. In situations that call for more technical knowledge of halakha, he'd reason through the alternative arguments and then conjure his *zeyde* (grandpa).

Sometimes matters require consultation. Shimen knows where to look in the books. For most matters, he'd consult the most widely accepted recent (early twentieth century) codes of Jewish law: the scholarly and dispassionate *Arukh HaShulḥan* and the more cautiously pious *Mishna Berura*, which themselves are based on the sixteenth-century code, *Shulḥan Arukh*, and dozens of commentaries thereon. The *Shulḥan Arukh* itself is based on earlier codes and commentaries, most prominently the twelfth-century code of Maimonides that is, in turn, distilled from the sprawling legal debates recorded in the Babylonian Talmud (third to sixth century) and the Jerusalem Talmud (third to fourth century), each of which is, in a loose sense, a commentary on the Mishna, the very first compilation[1] of post-biblical Jewish law.

Shimen isn't a sage who knows all this material by heart, but he is sufficiently well versed to navigate the literature quite easily when the need arises. Nevertheless, what Shimen finds in

---

1. The Mishna was "compiled" in the second century, though almost certainly transmitted orally for centuries before being committed to writing. The same is true of the Babylonian Talmud and the Jerusalem Talmud. See Y. Sussman, *"Oral Law" Taken Literally* [in Hebrew] (Jerusalem: Magnes Press, 2019).

the books is secondary to what he finds when he looks to his left and to his right in the *shtiebel*. When the author of the *Mishna Berura* writes, as he often does, that "the common practice is such and such, but this is wrong," Shimen's response is to credit the author's claim regarding the common practice and to ignore the admonition.

Sometimes Shimen will seek expert guidance. If he needs to make a particularly important personal decision, or to resolve a dispute with someone else, he'll consult an individual he trusts, usually a rabbi whose wisdom he respects. But, for the most part, in such cases he's looking not so much for a halakhic decision as for good advice, a fair compromise, or a bit of reassurance. He will also be interested in what the rabbis he respects have to say on matters of communal policy.

The problem is that the rabbis he respects were almost all murdered. There are a few rabbis among the survivors whom Shimen regards as worthy of being consulted. He considers most American rabbis worse than useless. The way Shimen sees it, their knowledge is from books, not from a living tradition; they are naive about the world and more immersed in shallow American culture than they realize; their opinions are either too lenient, because they are acculturated, or too stringent, because they are insecure about their own authenticity. In short, they are representative of American Orthodox Judaism, which for Shimen is nothing but a vulgar and superficial shadow of the authentic *Yiddishkeit* that he recalls with love and anguish.

To be precise, Shimen's definition of tradition is strictly bound not by what the books say or what the rabbis say or even what his friends actually do, but rather by his understanding of the native wisdom of people deeply immersed in the traditional way of life. Shimen made great efforts not to eat non-kosher food in the Lodz ghetto and yet now, perhaps unlike many of his friends in the *shtiebel*, Shimen would eat in the homes of those a bit less observant than he, without asking embarrassing questions. Shimen doesn't wear the hasidic clothing he wore before The War; under the circumstances, it would simply feel inauthentic, as if he were pretending that the world of Polish Hasidism had not been utterly destroyed. Shimen is more comfortable in the company of men, and most of the public events he attends are gender-segregated; yet he finds fair game for mockery in the stringent customs regarding separation of the sexes that have taken hold among Gerer Hasidim.

More generally, Shimen, like all of his friends in the *shtiebel*, doesn't have a need to signal his loyalty to the Jews through extravagant piety; he paid his dues up-front. If I might indulge in trifles, Shimen has no patience for *baalei keria* (those who lead public readings of the Torah) for whom the Torah reading is a tedious exercise in hyper-enunciation. If Shimen only had grandchildren, he'd undoubtedly kiss them during prayers, and God have mercy on the earnest yeshiva boy who'd point out to him that the codes forbid this.[2]

Shimen has no interest in justifying his stringencies or his leniencies, or in convincing others to accept them. He's completely comfortable in his own skin. He has no interest in sugarcoating Judaism to make it more palatable to those of refined taste. In fact, since for him Judaism is defined by tradition, the very idea of "fixing" it is inherently incoherent to him.

Below, we'll consider how halakha plays out in a community of Shimen's. How does the definition of tradition converge in a Keynesian beauty contest[3] – that is, one in which each person looks to the others to determine what the tradition is? If each person uses common sense to smooth the edges the way Shimen does, will halakha remain stable? How much power do rabbis really

---

2. *Shulḥan Arukh, Oraḥ Ḥayim* 98.
3. John Maynard Keynes, *The General Theory of Employment, Interest and Money* (New York: Harcourt Brace, 1936), chapter 12. Keynes compares stock-picking to a contest in which the challenge is to pick the picture that most contestants will find most attractive.

have in Shimen's world? How does halakha survive in the absence of legislation and enforcement?

Before we dive into these questions, we'll consider an alternative model for determining right and wrong that, unlike halakha, does depend on legislation and enforcement – namely, the model of Heidi's world.

HEIDI REJECTS SHIMEN'S DECISION METHODS

Since Heidi disagrees with Shimen regarding the substance of morality, it's no surprise that she also disagrees with him about the basis on which ethical and public policy questions should be decided, who should be making such decisions, and how they should be enforced.

Heidi rejects Shimen's obedience to tradition when modernity presents better solutions to problems that tradition solves sub-optimally. In Heidi's view, policy is best left to experts who master the latest research on the matters at hand. If we wish to avoid harmful foods, the modern study of nutrition offers much more efficient methods than the rules given in an ancient Torah. If we wish to strengthen families (and it isn't clear to Heidi that we should), psychologists and sex therapists can tell us how best to realize the human capacity for love and sexual fulfillment. If we wish to protect workers' rights, arcane Shabbat laws can't compete with the knowledge amassed by labor lawyers, social workers, and economists about the most efficient means for preventing human exploitation.

One can multiply such examples by the number of laws in the *Shulḥan Arukh*. The principle is the same each time: expertise, not tradition, is the key to a flourishing society.

To be sure, Shimen does not belittle expertise: when he's ill he goes to the best doctor he can find and when his sink leaks he calls a plumber. But when he needs guidance in resolving personal and social dilemmas, the only experts he seeks out – and not without misgivings, as we have seen above – are rabbis who can advise him according to the letter and spirit of halakha. This offers small solace to Heidi: These rabbis may know halakha, but what do they know about modern science, about history, about psychology and sociology? What tools do they have at their disposal that might help them respond sensibly and sensitively to those with serious personal problems, and what relevant knowledge do they possess that would allow them to shape public policy in any reasonably effective way?

As far as Heidi can tell, the vast majority of rabbis are both deficient in the relevant bodies of knowledge and socially inexperienced and naive. She suspects that they are often manipulated by hangers-on and sycophants with their own agendas.

The guidance of educated experts is, as Heidi sees it, to be preferred not only to tradition but to the half-baked intuitions of non-experts. Shimen, on the other hand, readily agrees that his determination of what is right is shaped by the moral intuitions of those committed to Jewish tradition. But for Heidi, if there's any worse guide to the healthy functioning of society than tradition, it surely must be the intuition of the masses. As the psychologists Daniel Kahneman and Amos Tversky demonstrate in a long series of experiments on the psychology of decision-making, intuition is hopelessly flawed as a basis for making decisions about anything, let alone moral questions.[4]

For example, our intuitive preferences between competing lottery scenarios don't maximize expected winnings but actually depend, quite absurdly, on how the scenarios are framed and other irrelevancies. In fact, our errors are systematic – we find patterns in randomness, we give more weight to evidence that stands out rather than to the most relevant evidence, we cling to our prior beliefs even in the face of strong contrary evidence, and so on. Such

---

4. Daniel Kahneman, *Thinking, Fast and Slow* (New York: Farrar, Straus and Giroux, 2011).

biases were presumably useful in the early days of human development, when snap decisions, even if only crude ones, were better than nothing. But, Heidi argues, many of the problems we face in modern societies can be better solved using the tools of logic and probability than relying on crude intuitions.

In fact, many of our cognitive biases bear directly on moral decisions: we make snap judgments about people based on largely irrelevant physical characteristics, we ascribe negative personality traits to people who don't share our opinions (even if we know that they were assigned that opinion as part of a debating exercise), we ascribe our own successes to skill and our failures to bad luck, we judge out-group members harshly even when the definition of our group is random, as with fans of some sports teams or members of a color-war team in a summer camp.[5] Heidi is convinced that if, instead of following their misleading intuitions about such matters, Shimen and Jews like him would take a deep breath and reason about their loyalties, they would surely treat outsiders more fairly.

In short, although Heidi can't deny that most of her political positions are rooted in her own intuitions, she still believes that, in principle, the decisions that drive public policy should be taken by experts and not on the basis of either tradition or intuition.

Heidi also differs from Shimen on an even more fundamental point. Once some policies have been determined to be worth pursuing, who should be responsible for implementing and enforcing them? In Heidi's world, one with loose communal affiliations, state agencies implement and enforce policy. In fact, Heidi very naturally divides norms into two types: those that are legislated and enforced (or ought to be) and those that are simply not obligatory. But, it seems to her, in Shimen's world, with its tight-knit communities,

---

5. M. Sherif, O. J. Harvey, B. J. White, W. R. Hood, and C. W. Sherif, *Intergroup Conflict and Cooperation: The Robbers Cave Experiment* (Norman, OK: University Book Exchange, 1961).

social norms fail to fit into either category. They are neither legislated nor enforced, and yet they are somehow regarded as obligatory. Heidi regards this as a double failure. First, as we saw above, halakha regards as obligatory constraints and duties in areas that should, in Heidi's view, be left to personal discretion. Second, halakha fails to adequately address issues that are, for Heidi, essential to the functioning of society. It lacks both the necessary mechanisms to resolve disagreements regarding proper practice and the means necessary for enforcing the rules.

Heidi's claim about the lack of mechanisms to resolve halakhic disputes certainly has a strong basis. In the very first recorded halakhic dispute, more than 2,100 years ago, five consecutive generations of rabbis failed to agree on the procedure for bringing certain sacrifices on Festivals.[6] From that point on, the entire corpus of halakhic literature is, as every novice student knows, an unending series of disputes. What is the proper blessing before eating chocolate? At what time of day should one light Ḥanukka candles? Can cooked food be put on a hotplate on Shabbat? What is the minimum age for a rabbinic judge? Is a brain-dead person with a beating heart considered dead? Does halakha recognize intellectual property rights?

Ask a rabbi any of these questions and thousands more like them, and the inevitable answer will be "It's a *maḥloket*," a matter of rabbinic dispute. This is not (only) because rabbis are particularly argumentative, but rather because halakha lacks a formal mechanism for resolving disputes, at least for the past two thousand or so years.

Heidi's second contention, that halakha lacks enforcement mechanisms, is also true. Of course, there are many issues, such as matters of criminal law, that Shimen concedes are beyond the capacity of current halakha to deal with. In this regard, halakha is plainly not

---

6. Mishna Ḥagiga 2:2.

self-contained but takes for granted the authority of an exogenous power that deals with matters beyond its scope. But Heidi is bothered by what she regards as a more egregious failure of halakha. Shimen and his friends seem to wish to handle at the communal level certain issues that Heidi believes can be better addressed by the state, which has the means of implementing the necessary remedies.

Compare, for example, how the problem of poverty is addressed by individual and community charity on the one hand, and by the state welfare system on the other hand. Halakha requires individuals to set aside 10 percent of their income for charity, but doesn't specify to whom it should be given. What guarantee is there that all poor people will receive sufficient charity? What grounds are there for supposing that all will meet their obligations in the absence of any sanctions? Who will take care of those who belong to poor communities or to no community at all?

For Heidi, these are serious defects that can be remedied: the state should redistribute wealth by collecting taxes (at the threat of imprisonment) and providing entitlements such as welfare, free health care, and unemployment benefits. The state can further advance the cause of social justice through regulation, including rent control, anti-discrimination laws, and labor laws; these are all favored by Heidi as means through which the powerful and wealthy are prevented from exploiting the weak and poor.

To Heidi, the belief of Shimen and his friends that their moral world ends at the boundaries of their narrow community is a moral failing. It is a mystery to her that after all the suffering they have seen, they remain almost entirely indifferent to the astonishing ability of the welfare state, guided by the best experts in the social sciences, to engineer a more perfect society.

We'll have opportunity below to consider whether Heidi's confidence in the welfare state is justified. But first let's try to get a better grasp on halakha. If it's not a product of the deliberate efforts of legislators, how exactly does it develop?

Chapter 6

Between Law and Language

Heidi's claims regarding the differences between halakha and modern legal systems are straightforward, and, as a first approximation, indisputable. Unlike modern legal systems, halakha is indeed deeply rooted in entrenched traditions and lacks a mechanism for legislating changes, it relies on the intuitions of ordinary practitioners of halakha, and it lacks a systematic means of enforcement.

Building on her factual claims, however, Heidi also makes some evaluative claims. Since halakha lacks a mechanism to overcome old traditions, she concludes, it must inevitably become stale and outdated. This defect is exacerbated by the lack of a mechanism for legislation, which prevents responsiveness even to acute need for reform. Furthermore, in the absence of legislation, halakha remains poorly defined, lacking both precision and consensus. Relying on often-flawed intuitions, it is also vulnerable to systemic bias. Since Shimen's intuition is rooted in what his neighbors do and theirs is rooted in what he does, the outcome is bound to be both unstable and greatly variable from place to place. Finally, since halakha is unenforced, it is bound to fray at the margins, and thus to fail to achieve even its own goals.

Do Heidi's evaluative claims follow analytically from her factual claims? Even if we knew nothing about halakha's successes and failures, we could prove that they do not. That's because there is a phenomenon unrelated to halakha that satisfies every one of Heidi's factual claims about halakha and yet clearly does not suffer from any of the failures predicted by the evaluative claims.

I'm talking about language.

LANGUAGE ISN'T LEGISLATED OR ENFORCED

Every language is deeply rooted in entrenched practices and lacks a mechanism for legislation. (Yes, some especially enthusiastic countries have august National Academies for regulating the local tongue; they're usually about as effective as cat-herders.) Every language relies on the linguistic intuitions of the masses of its speakers, and every language lacks a systematic means of enforcement.[1]

And yet, languages work just fine. They don't become stale or outdated. Even without the oversight of august academies, they adapt perfectly well to the needs of speakers and writers. Nameless new phenomena magically get names, like *googling* or *crowdsourcing*, both of which can be used to assemble a list of many more such neologisms. The meanings of many words gradually change over time. Some viewers of TV reruns are startled by the stone-age Flintstones having a gay old time, which just proves these viewers aren't woke. Moreover, many old words, like *well* and *so*, are repurposed to serve pragmatic roles rather than semantic ones. (Well, maybe that point is a bit arcane, so let's move on.)

---

1. See Steven Pinker, *The Language Instinct: How the Mind Creates Language* (New York: William Morrow, 1994).

Anyway, if you believe that language is static, try your hand at the Canterbury Tales, allegedly written in a form of English.

Unlike the case of law, all those changes are brought about without any visible hand guiding the development of language. We might say, following the Scottish philosopher Adam Ferguson and the Austrian economist F. A. Hayek, that the development of language is the result of human action but not of human design.[2] Moreover, the humans performing these actions are just regular people speaking and writing intuitively, not fancy experts who've researched the rules.

It is remarkable how competent we are at using our native languages; we know intuitively much more than we realize we know. To appreciate this point, please look right over there at that wooden, blue, big box... Whoa, that sounded weird. You know why? Because everybody knows that it should be "big, blue, wooden box." The order has to be size, color, material. The beautiful thing about that is that everybody knows it, but almost nobody knows that they know it. Intuition works.

Finally, unlike in the case of law, the rules of language aren't enforced by the state or by any other duly constituted body that can fine or imprison us for breaking the rules. Nevertheless, most people choose to follow the rules well enough to make themselves understood.

In short, language differs from law in many of the same ways that halakha differs from law: a certain stodginess, vulnerability to the whims of the great unwashed, and the lack of a parliament and a police force. And yet it gets the job done.

HALAKHA RUNS ALONG TWO TRACKS

Careful consideration of how halakha actually operates on the ground, combined with an analysis of the idealized version of

---

2. Adam Ferguson, *An Essay on the History of Civil Society* (London, UK: T. Cadell, 1767); F. A. Hayek, "The Results of Human Action but Not of Human Design," in *Studies in Philosophy, Politics and Economics* 96 (1967).

halakha found in the rabbinic literature, suggests that halakha lies on a continuum between language and law.

We can begin by comparing halakha with law and with language on the dimension of enforcement. Matters of law are typically adjudicated and enforced by the government that legislated the laws; violators can be fined or imprisoned by agencies of the state. Matters of language, on the other hand, are adjudicated and enforced by rather benign editors, if at all. Miscreants who brazenly split infinitives might suffer a loss of prestige if their infractions are interpreted as the result of ineptitude or poor socialization, but they can remain fairly confident that no posse will come after them. The desire to be understood and to be taken seriously is generally a sufficient incentive for writers and speakers more or less to follow the rules.

Halakha lies somewhere between these extremes. For the past two millennia, since the end of Jewish autonomy in ancient Israel,[3] matters of halakha have for the most part been adjudicated by rabbis consulted on a voluntary basis and have been enforced almost solely by social pressure, which – as deeply unpleasant as it sometimes is – does not rise to the level of imprisonment in a federal penitentiary.

Now let's compare halakha to law and to language along the axis of legislation. If Shimen wants to know what the American law is with regard to some matter or other, he can look it up

---

3. It might legitimately be objected that the Torah regards as an ideal a central authority that legislates and enforces Jewish law, including the death penalty, and that such an authority did in fact exist at various times. Nevertheless, such enforcement petered out for social and political reasons already well prior to the destruction of the Second Temple, and the Sanhedrin ceased to function as a quasi-legislative body at some point following the Bar Kokhba revolt. Thus, the absence of legislation and enforcement (apart from narrow communal affairs) can be regarded as a natural and firmly entrenched property of halakha as it has been practiced for about two millennia and as it is likely to remain under foreseeable circumstances.

in the official statutes code that records acts of the legislature. These official codes don't merely reflect the law; they are actually constitutive. On the other hand, language is not legislated. If Shimen wants to know how to speak English properly, he can just pay attention to the way everybody else speaks. He might find it convenient to check what the grammar textbooks or websites have to say, but those aren't constitutive; they are useful simply because they reflect common practice.

How would Shimen decide "what the halakha is" in some instance? Can he look it up in some constitutive codes, as he might with legislation, or should he just do what people do, as he would with language? One answer, only slightly too clever, is that most codes would say to do what people do and most people will say to follow the codes. The implications of these two independent claims will be central to the rest of this part of the book, but for now it is sufficient simply to say that halakha develops along two tracks that can't diverge by much because from time to time they need to intersect.

One of these tracks looks a bit like law. Faced with a matter that requires a halakhic ruling, scholars argue the merits of each possibility, citing analogies with related cases, weighing conflicting principles, and pondering the likely consequences of a given ruling on the affected parties and on the integrity of the system. These discussions are recorded in, among other places, commentaries on earlier legal works and responses to legal questions addressed to authorities. These discussions and rulings resemble case law (rulings by judges that rely heavily on precedent) rather than statutory law (legislation). Occasionally, the accretion of such rulings is distilled and summarized in a halakhic code like that of Maimonides or the *Shulḥan Arukh*.

Such codes resemble statutory law in the sense that they are expressed as general principles of law rather than as rulings regarding specific cases. But they differ from typical statutory law in two crucial ways: they are not produced by a legislature but rather by an individual without recognized institutional authority, and, unlike legislation, they can't change established law. Nevertheless, the most important codes are so influential that many people think of them as constitutive.

The other track looks a bit like language. Faced with a subtle everyday situation for which there is no obvious established practice, those committed to and knowledgeable in tradition tentatively act according to their intuitions while carefully watching what others do in similar situations. As in the case of language, this apparently circular process somehow manages eventually to converge in some consensus practice. The emergent consensus is regarded by many people as constitutive.

Separating out these two processes – intuitive practice and deliberative codification – is convenient for expository purposes but somewhat misleading. In fact, the two tracks are strongly interdependent, and periodically and necessarily coalesce.

First of all, the "language" track draws on codification. When we speak of our halakhic intuitions, we mean intuitions rooted in knowledge of established halakha. Nobody, not even Shimen, is born with intuition regarding, for example, the laws of separating the bones from the flesh of a fish at Shabbat dinner; rather, given knowledge of related laws, one might develop some sense of what is permissible in a given situation. Such prior knowledge could in principle be drawn from observing common practice, but in fact is often drawn from studying the relevant literature. Similarly, when Shimen emulates his neighbors, he gives little weight to those who are ignorant of or uncommitted to established traditions and a great deal of weight to those who are highly knowledgeable and committed. The codes are a convenient touchstone for measuring these qualities. Note, though, that both the need for prior knowledge and the need for identifying reliable practitioners hold in the case of language as well – and languages manage without codes.

Conversely, the halakhic literature can't actually be constitutive independently of common practice. In fact, the codes draw strongly on actual practice. For example, the *Shulḥan Arukh* frequently cites multiple possible rulings regarding a given situation and then resolves the matter by noting that the practice is in accord with a particular one. The startling implication of such a statement is that a *popular* consensus has formed prior to a *rabbinic* consensus. Even Maimonides, who records only a single ruling regarding any given situation, defers to common practice as being decisive.[4] Moreover, since no code has institutional authority in the way that a legislature does, the authority of any given code is itself entirely dependent on its broad acceptance. Why are the rulings of the *Shulḥan Arukh* more decisive than those of any one of dozens of other codes? Only because this particular code has gained especially broad acceptance. In this sense, the last word remains with popular sentiment.

To summarize the process, then, some prior body of halakhic knowledge, as summarized in the codes and other halakhic literature, serves as a foundation for individual intuition that, in aggregate, converges to consensus on various issues not covered by the extant body of halakhic knowledge. These consensus practices are then incorporated into rulings and codes that serve as the expanded body of halakhic knowledge, on the basis of which the process continues.

In sum, the codes reflect practice and practice reflects the codes.

HALAKHA AS A FIRST LANGUAGE

The analogy between language and halakha is obvious to Shimen. He experiences them in the same way: both were learned

---

4. Maimonides, *Mishneh Torah, Hilkhot Shemitta VeYovel* [Laws of Sabbatical and Jubilee Years] 10:6.

mainly mimetically; both are practiced intuitively; and both are communal phenomena. But for a typical American yeshiva student of Heidi's generation – let's call him Yitzy – the analogy between language and halakha is perplexing. He learned halakha from books, he practices it by navigating an obstacle course of seemingly arbitrary rules, and he is irritated by the propensity of his parents' community to get so many things wrong.

The difference between Shimen and Yitzy is that Shimen speaks halakha as a first language and Yitzy speaks it as a second language. A first language is spoken fluently and intuitively without much conscious attention to the rules. A second language is spoken haltingly and stiltedly, as part of the mind is occupied with retrieving the relevant learned rule.

There are many good sociological reasons for halakha's having become a second language for many of its practitioners, a phenomenon I'll discuss later in the book. At this stage, I want to make a single point that I'm afraid is completely lost on Yitzy: halakha is meant to be spoken as a first language, not as a second language. To celebrate the shift of halakhic knowledge from people's minds to their books is to make a virtue of necessity.

I'll make this point in two different ways. On the theoretical side, the main written sources of Jewish tradition themselves repeatedly make the point that halakha is *ideally* meant to be spoken fluently like a first language and not learned from written rules like a second language. On the practical side, many examples of halakhic development demonstrate that laws in written halakhic codes reflect common practice rather than the other way around.

The Talmud itself[5] records the undisputed opinion of R. Yehuda bar Naḥmani, a third-century scholar in the Land of Israel,

5. Gittin 60b.

that no Jewish text other than the Bible should be written: "That which was transmitted orally you are not permitted to write." The oral tradition was compiled and subsequently committed to writing only when social turmoil threatened its very existence. Elaborating on this point, a midrash[6] tells of Moses's request of God at Sinai that the Oral Law transmitted to him in conjunction with the Torah be written down as well. God refuses, explaining that what is written can be copied and imitated by other nations, but the oral tradition will uniquely define the Jewish people; that is, native speakers of the language will always be distinguishable from those who speak by the rules, without nuance.

A number of stories related in the Talmud focus on the crisis-driven replacement of intuitive understanding of the Oral Law by formal rules. The Talmud[7] reports that after Moses died, taking with him his uniquely intuitive understanding of Torah, the Law had to be reconstructed by Othniel ben Kenaz (the first leader of the Jews not present at Sinai) using formal methods. Such reconstructions are reported[8] as having been undertaken by a number of transitional leaders, including Ezra the Scribe and Hillel the Elder, during periods of crisis. And it is Hillel the Elder who, when faced with a halakhic conundrum that the leading rabbis could not solve, is reported[9] to have responded, "Let the Jews decide, for if they aren't prophets, they are the children of prophets."

In a related legend,[10] Moses travels almost two millennia forward in time to the school of Rabbi Akiva and finds the discussion bewilderingly unfamiliar, only to be informed that the laws under discussion originate with Moses himself. To an intuitive speaker of a language, the rules of grammar that are taught to those acquiring

---

6. Shemot Rabba 47:1.
7. Temura 16a.
8. Sukka 20a.
9. Pesaḥim 66a.
10. Menaḥot 29b.

the language in a school are often strange and mystifying, even though the students are in fact acquiring his own native language.

Each of these stories makes the same point. Intuitive knowledge of Torah (Torah as a first language) is replaced by a compiled set of rules (Torah as an acquired language) only when necessary.

In fact, as Yitzy would surely be surprised to hear, each of the major codifications of Jewish law was resisted by leading scholars of the time, who feared ossification of halakha. Thus, for example, Rabbi Judah Loew of Prague, a leading sixteenth-century Jewish thinker known as Maharal, opposed the publication of the *Shulḥan Arukh* (literally, "the set table"), arguing that "we ought not rely on parchment...the Torah should be in our mouths, not on the table."[11]

Maharal's fears might have been somewhat exaggerated. As we've seen, codes like the *Shulḥan Arukh* actually reflect popular practices more than they determine them, and are incapable of preventing popular disinclination to abide by their rulings. In a considerable number of cases, rulings cited in the codes lose general support and subsequent codes reflect the later practice.

Consider, for example, the following once-common halakhic practices that eventually became counter-intuitive: mourners stopped wearing hoods ("it makes us look ridiculous to the gentiles"),[12] and their visitors stopped sitting on the ground with them; unmarried women stopped covering their hair as a sign of modesty; penitents stopped submitting to lashes on the eve of Yom Kippur. Another practice on Yom Kippur eve serves as an interesting contrast to this last example: despite the disapproval of the *Shulḥan Arukh*,[13] the ritual of *kaparot* – slaughtering a chicken as penance – remained popular to the extent that

---

11. Maharal, Appendix to *Be'er HaGola*.
12. *Beit Yosef, Yoreh De'ah* 386, citing *Hagahot Maimoniyot*.
13. *Shulḥan Arukh, Oraḥ Ḥayim* 605.

this disapproval was deleted in later editions of the book. In fact, in all the cases mentioned here, all contemporary codes reflect the later practice.

When new issues arise, popular consensus often precedes rabbinic consensus. For example, turkey was almost universally regarded as a kosher bird long before rabbis made any determination to that effect. Conversely, gelatin made from the bones of non-kosher animals was almost universally regarded as non-kosher, despite significant rabbinic support for its permissibility.

It might be instructive to think of the power of rabbis to establish halakha as something like the power of merchants to set prices. It looks to all the world as if merchants are free to set prices as they wish. In fact, however, supply and demand determine a very narrow range of supportable prices.

The use of technologies on Shabbat is an area rife with examples of rabbis leading from behind. Electricity came into wide use in urban areas in the 1880s. The first to rule against the permissibility of the use of electric devices on Shabbat was the rabbi of Lemberg, Rabbi Isaac Shmelkes, in 1895.[14] He argued that creating a new electric current was somehow akin to transferring fragrance, which the Talmud forbids on somewhat vague grounds. This prohibition was universally accepted, as evidenced by the fact that almost all subsequent scholars take the prohibition as a given despite rejecting the reasoning behind it. But lest the reader think that it was Rabbi Shmelkes's authority that determined the popular practice, consider that in the very same responsum he employed the identical reasoning to prohibit carbonating water, a prohibition honored by exactly nobody. Evidently, it was not the ruling that determined the practice, but rather the widespread sense that electricity was a bigger threat to Shabbat than seltzer.

---

14. *Beit Yitzḥak, Yoreh De'ah* 2:31.

Similarly, Rabbi Moshe Feinstein, recognized almost universally as the leading halakhic expert in the United States from the 1950s through the 1970s, ruled that the use of liquid soap on Shabbat is prohibited,[15] extending Rabbi Shmelkes's argument to the creation of bubbles. This one never caught on. On the other hand, Rabbi Feinstein broadly hints in several rulings that extinguishing gas burners on Festivals (and, reading between the lines, possibly on Shabbat) may not be prohibited at all, but he is plainly unwilling to state this publicly, presumably because he regarded this as a leniency the public could not bear. Contemporary codes reflect the common practice, not the rulings of the leading rabbi of the past generation.

Finally, those of us who have been alive long enough have seen customs change before our very eyes. The *Hoshanot* ritual (circling of the synagogue hall during the Sukkot prayer service), according to the Ashkenazi custom, was traditionally placed at the end of the service; this somewhat inconvenient tradition is slowly disappearing in favor of performing it earlier in the service, despite no rabbinic rulings on the matter. Similarly, the blowing of the shofar during the silent *Musaf* prayer on Rosh HaShana, the standard practice according to the hasidic custom, seems to be rapidly losing popularity, despite there being no ruling to this effect.

Another, somewhat esoteric, example is the current American *yeshivish* custom for those who are seated at a wedding ceremony to stand as the groom and then the bride pass by. Yitzy, who earnestly practices this sacred rite, will be shocked to learn that it was completely unheard of as recently as a single generation ago. Leading American rabbis have now begun weighing in on the matter, manufacturing several unconvincing grounds for

---

15. *Iggerot Moshe, Oraḥ Ḥayim* 1:113.

the practice (presumably not including adherents having seen too many church weddings on TV).

In short, in an ideal world, halakha is meant to be uncodified, like the rules of grammar, precisely so that its practice remain fluid much the way a native language is spoken. In the real world, codification is often necessary to prevent too much drift during times when collective intuition is compromised; in such cases codification typically reflects the common practice more than it engenders it.

This blend of bottom-up and top-down development is, as we shall see presently, responsible for halakha's adaptiveness.

Chapter 7

The Need for Tradition

Now that we have some understanding of how halakha works, let's consider the advantages that this mechanism yields for halakha's continued viability. We'll split the argument into four parts. First, we'll see the advantages of respecting traditions generally. Then we'll consider the specific advantages of the fact that halakha balances intuition and codification. Next, we'll look at the benefits of the particular way in which halakha aggregates the opinions of experts and non-experts. Finally, we'll consider the reasons for preferring that this entire process take place within an appropriately defined community rather than, for example, among the citizens of a state.

RESPECTING ESTABLISHED CUSTOMS

Old Hasidim like Shimen and young *yeshivish* types like Yitzy might quibble about the weight we ought to give to popular custom relative to written codes, but, unlike Heidi, they agree that we ought to be very cautious about casually discarding established norms.

Let's consider the advantages of fidelity to received tradition – whether popular or formalized – for the long-term viability of a society. The essence of the argument is painfully simple: social norms that have kept a community going are likelier to keep it going than ones that haven't. Let's start with a homely example. Do you like tapioca? Me neither. It comes from the root of the cassava plant, which is one of the main sources of starch in the South American diet. Cassava root is similar to sweet potato and is one of the root vegetables they use for making those funny-colored potato chip wannabes (often sold under the Spanish name *yucca*, a stroke of marketing genius). South American tribes have been cultivating cassava for millennia and have developed rather complicated and painstaking methods for preparing it for consumption. For example, the anthropologist Joseph Henrich reports[1] that the Tukanoans in the Colombian Amazon use a process involving scraping, grating, washing, boiling, drying for several days, and finally baking. If, as Henrich did, you ask them why they go through this complicated rigmarole, they'll tell you that it's simply their tradition.

When consumption of cassava spread to West Africa in the eighteenth century, the traditional methods for preparing it did not always follow. Which, as it turns out, is quite a pity. But there is no way that someone not armed with modern knowledge of food chemistry and toxicology could possibly have anticipated the high incidence of goiters and leg paralysis that developed years later in those parts of Africa, and that persist until today, all as a result of the consumption of unprocessed cassava root.

The Tukanoans were not aware, and could not have been aware, of the connection between their rituals and the prevention of cyanide poisoning that in the long term was responsible for the symptoms. The ritual developed in the distant past among some

---

1. Henrich, *The Secret of Our Success*, 97–100.

of their ancestors for whatever reason (or for no reason), and proliferated from there, presumably because young people have a slight preference – or maybe more opportunity – for learning rituals from people without goiters and leg paralysis.

I do not mean to infer from this example that traditions typically have some direct salutary effect on public health. Rather, the lesson is that particular social norms proliferate and survive within a society because, as we saw earlier, they contribute to the society's survival, even if no member of that society actually understands exactly how they do so. As F. A. Hayek puts it: "The cultural heritage into which man is born consists of a complex of practices or rules of conduct which have prevailed because they made a group of men successful but which were not adopted because it was known that they would bring about desired effects."[2] We discard such traditions at our peril.

Heidi might respond, quite reasonably, that this makes good sense for Tukanoans only so long as they lack the requisite scientific knowledge and remain unaware of methods for cultivating species of cassava low in cyanide. Once they would learn such methods, their traditions would be nothing but a drag on resources, and they'd be wise to abandon them.

This is a strong argument. But it rests on the assumption that we can retrospectively understand precisely how a given tradition contributes to a society's long-term viability. In fact, systems of social norms are delicate mechanisms; attempts to demystify them are inherently speculative, and attempts to improve them can be dangerous.

For example, Tukanoans who sensibly switched to cultivating sweet cassava, which is low in cyanide, would discover that the lack of cyanide made the root vegetable more attractive to both pests and thieves, and that the diminished need for processing

---

2. F. A. Hayek, *Law, Legislation and Liberty*, vol. 1 (Oxfordshire, UK: Routledge, 1973), 17.

cassava lowered the status of women, whose primary contribution to the society was doing just that. More generally, they would also discover that discarding one tradition leads to weakening respect for other traditions for which there are no efficient alternatives. The point is not that it is always worth maintaining every tradition; folk medicine, for example, certainly leaves room for improvement. Rather, abandoning traditions that have proven to be useful for reasons that we don't understand is likely to lead to consequences that we don't anticipate. For a particularly salient contemporary example: before embarking on a massive, and possibly irreversible, social experiment based on the abandonment of the very idea of gender dichotomy, a society would be well advised to ask itself if it's feeling lucky enough to be rolling those dice.

I emphasize again that I'm not making a claim here regarding which traditions are morally superior but rather which traditions are essential for a society's viability. But if a society doesn't survive, it probably will not be doing much good.

Of course, as circumstances change, taking traditions too seriously could itself be harmful. After all, received traditions have not been around forever but are rather the unanticipated result of subtle innovations that proved in retrospect to have staying power. Failing to adapt at all is exceedingly maladaptive. In fact, perfect traditionalism is poorly defined to the point of paradox. Suppose some new custom has spread in the past generation – say, standing up for a bride and groom. Would the perfect conservative reject the newfangled custom in favor of that old-time religion or adopt the later tradition as he received it? How entrenched must a custom be before it becomes a member in good standing of that old-time religion? Curmudgeonliness alone can't be the answer.

Preserving tradition while maintaining adaptiveness is a delicate matter. It requires mechanisms for handling subtle trade-offs, including balancing both moral intuition with conscious reasoning, and popular practice with elite leadership. In what follows, we'll consider some of the mechanisms that traditional Judaism has developed for just this purpose.

INTUITION AND CODIFICATION

Rabbi Avraham Yeshaya Karelitz, commonly known as Ḥazon Ish (the name of his main literary work), was widely regarded as the leading talmudic thinker in Israel in the 1940s and early 1950s. In a work[3] published in 1953, the year of his death, he considers the following problem: a projectile is on target to hit and kill a crowd of people, but some observer is in a position to deflect it so that the crowd would be saved but some other bystander would be killed. In considering whether the observer should indeed deflect the projectile, Ḥazon Ish cites a case discussed in the Mishna in which a group of hostages are threatened with death unless they hand over a random member of the group to be killed.[4] The Mishna rules that it is forbidden for the group to save themselves by giving up one of the members. Ḥazon Ish argues that, the Mishna's ruling notwithstanding, one *could* nevertheless deflect the projectile because the cases are concretely different: in the case of the projectile, deflection is a positive act with a negative consequence, and hence permitted, while in the case of the hostages, the handing over of one hostage is a negative act with a positive consequence, and hence forbidden. (This distinction is at the core of the "doctrine of double effect" attributed to the medieval religious thinker Thomas Aquinas.)

In 1967, the British philosopher Phillipa Foot published an oft-quoted paper[5] comparing two cases identical in substance to those raised by Ḥazon Ish. Subsequently, the philosopher Judith

---

3. A. Y. Karelitz, *Ḥazon Ish*, Glosses on Tractate Sanhedrin, Section 25 (1953).
4. Mishna Terumot 8:4.
5. Philippa Foot, "The Problem of Abortion and the Doctrine of Double Effect," *Oxford Review* 5 (1967): 5–15.

Jarvis Thompson popularized[6] these dilemmas in the form of what are now known as "trolley problems."

In Thompson's version, a trolley is on course to run over five maintenance workers on the tracks. In one case, an observer is in position to pull a lever to steer it off course so that it would spare the workers but kill one other person instead. In another case, an observer can push a fat man off a bridge onto the tracks, thereby killing him but stopping the trolley from killing the five workers. Most people confronted with these problems favor pulling the lever, but not pushing the fat man – or at least that's what they tell the grad student asking the funny questions.

Trolley problems have become popular because they are a convenient way to test people's intuitions about basic moral dilemmas. If we are prone to resolve such dilemmas based solely on the consequences of our decisions (that is, if we are "consequentialists"), there should be little difference between pushing the fat man and pulling the lever: in either case we save five people by sacrificing one person. On the other hand, if we are prone to forbid or require particular actions based on certain rigid principles regardless of the consequences (that is, if we are "deontologists"), we might – depending on what those rigid principles are – permit pulling the lever but forbid pushing the fat man.

Deontologists like to point out the folly of particular versions of consequentialism – such as utilitarianism, which resolves moral dilemmas by tallying the overall utility to society – by noting that such reasoning would lead to the conclusion that a healthy young man visiting a hospital could be killed for his body parts if they could be used to save the lives of multiple patients in the hospital. Consequentialists counter by citing particular versions

6. J. J. Thomson, "The Trolley Problem," *The Yale Law Journal* 94 no. 6 (1985): 1395–1415. For a popular overview of the literature, see T. Cathcart, *The Trolley Problem, or Would You Throw the Fat Guy Off the Bridge? A Philosophical Conundrum* (New York: Workman Publishing, 2013).

of deontology, such as Kantianism, that require that one never lie, even if it means telling the Nazi at the door that Anne Frank is up in the attic. (To which some Kantians would respond, "Yeah, so?" – which is what makes them so endearing.) For these reasons, most normal people are neither strict utilitarians nor strict Kantians.[7] Why are trolley problems interesting? Because they pit our intuitive visceral sense that some things are no-nos against our reasoning about optimizing consequences. The philosopher-neurobiologist Joshua Greene has even shown that the two processes actually activate different parts of our brain.[8] Thus, while the vast majority of people assert that pulling the lever is right and pushing the fat man is wrong, people with damage to the ventromedial prefrontal cortex, the part of the brain where emotions and moral decision-making interact, are more likely to favor pushing the fat man.

And why am I telling you all this? Because it allows us some insight into how and why intuition and reasoning interact to resolve borderline halakhic issues.

Moral intuition is inescapable. Both Kantians and consequentialists imagine themselves, astonishingly, to be in possession of some formula that resolves moral dilemmas without the need to appeal to intuition. Yet they try to persuade each other precisely by invoking moral intuition: "Surely you wouldn't carve up the healthy visitor for body parts!" or "Surely you wouldn't cough up Anne Frank to the Nazis!" These "surely" arguments are surely nothing but naked appeals to intuition. Similarly, a consequentialist might coolly compute what action

---

7. For an accessible presentation of the deontologist-consequentialist debates and related issues, see M. Sandel, *Justice: What's the Right Thing to Do?* (New York: Farrar, Straus and Giroux, 2009).

8. Joshua D. Greene, Leigh E. Nystrom, Andrew D. Engell, John M. Darley, and Jonathan D. Cohen, "The Neural Bases of Cognitive Conflict and Control in Moral Judgment," *Neuron* 44, no. 2 (2004): 389–400.

in some given circumstance would maximize some quantity – in the case of trolley problems, probably the number of lives saved – but he first needs to decide intuitively what it is he wishes to maximize.

To see this point more starkly, let's revisit those poor souls with damage to the ventromedial prefrontal cortex. Their preference for pushing the fat man to save five lives might suggest that they are a bunch of hyper-rational Mr. Spocks not seduced by misleading emotions in the guise of intuition. Should we contemplate emulating them? Well, it turns out, as in a series of studies by the neurologist Antonio Damasio, that these people actually live wretched lives characterized by an inability to make the most elementary social decisions or to manage risk and ambiguity. Without some emotional basis for deciding what it is they want to optimize, they're as stuck as deer in headlights.[9]

Intuition, then, is necessary. But it is not sufficient.

Consider the approach of Ḥazon Ish to the projectile problem. Ḥazon Ish takes as his starting point those principles already established as normative. These principles include the ruling of the Mishna prohibiting handing over a hostage, as well as related principles suggested by later commentators. He suggests an intuitive difference between the hostage case and the projectile case; this intuition is almost universal, as recent wide-scale studies on trolley problems suggest. Ḥazon Ish then translates this intuition into a rule that hinges on whether the resulting deaths are a direct consequence of the contemplated act or mere collateral damage of a defensive maneuver. (He does not suggest that this is the only relevant criterion, and indeed, philosophers raise numerous other possible criteria that Ḥazon Ish might very well have accepted as relevant.)

---

9. A. R. Damasio, *Descartes' Error: Emotion, Reason, and the Human Brain* (New York: Grosset/Putnam, 1994).

Now, if we would, in any event, collectively reach the same conclusion as Ḥazon Ish based on our intuition, what advantage is there in deferring to rabbinic analysis of the sort that Ḥazon Ish and his colleagues offer? Why could we not proceed as we do in speaking our native language, employing intuitively understood rules without ever bothering to formalize them? After all, translating our intuition into rules is like casting a net and ensnaring a fragile and fleeting bird; in so doing, halakha becomes something of a second language, as we saw earlier.

Well, we do pay a price for formalizing halakhic intuition; but we gain a great deal as well.

First of all, one can easily construct intermediate cases – say, diverting the train saves five people but kills four bystanders, or kills a relative – where most people don't have any clear intuition. A theory of trolley decisions can serve us well in such cases. More broadly, then, articulated principles of halakha serve us when we don't have clear intuitions on the matter at hand.

Also, rules are easier to preserve than intuitions. Thus, under traumatic conditions – persecution, exile, dispersion, the sorts of things that befall Jews from time to time – when collective memory is likely to fail us, clear rules are more likely to remain stable than vague intuitions, especially if the rules are committed to writing. This is the meaning of the talmudic stories we saw earlier regarding the reconstruction of halakha during periods of upheaval.

Furthermore, the process of formulating clear principles helps us overcome systemic bias. For example, we might each be more prone to push the fat man if, say, he speaks with a funny accent or is otherwise unappealing in some irrelevant way; the need to reason through our actions forces us to overcome such biases. Or we might be less prone to push the fat man because our empathy for someone who happens to be in our vicinity is stronger than our empathy for five people whose faces we can't see, a fact that detached reflection might suggest should not be relevant to our decision.

More generally, we can be easily misled because our basic moral intuitions are rooted in small-scale communities of people for whom we feel great empathy, rather than in large societies of people with most of whom we share neither kinship nor friendship. But, in order that our commercial and social dealings with an ever-widening circle of strangers operate efficiently, we are less in need of empathy than we are of clear rules of exchange. That's why social norms are often designed to facilitate such impersonal interactions precisely when, as Hayek puts it, we have "to restrain some good instincts to develop the extended order."[10]

In short, in dealing with cases at the borderline of tradition, we have no choice but to employ both intuition and reasoned formalization of that intuition. But, where halakhic Judaism is concerned, there are also independent reasons to combine popular consensus with rabbinic guidance, as we shall now see.

AGGREGATING VOTES

I wrote above that for Shimen, Judaism is defined by tradition, so the very idea of "fixing" it is inherently incoherent to him. That glib formulation might suggest to some readers that halakha is whatever observant Jews practice, so that it is impossible by definition for such practice to be wrong. That understanding is mistaken. If Shimen were to wake up in a hundred years to discover that human sacrifice had become a venerable tradition in certain circles that claimed to be practicing halakha, he assuredly wouldn't respond with a resigned shrug of his shoulders. Shimen

---

10. F. A. Hayek, *The Fatal Conceit: The Errors of Socialism* (Oxfordshire, UK: Routledge, 1988), 13. Hayek distinguishes between small circles of kin and friends, among whom formal norms are unnecessary because empathy and other tribal instincts suffice, and large societies, in which empathy and tribal instincts must be suppressed in favor of formal norms. The communities of which I speak are intermediate between these and invoke both tribal instincts and social norms. Small circles are bounded in size by what is known as the Dunbar number (roughly 150), while the maximum size of the communities of which I speak is probably about two orders of magnitude greater.

knows that tradition is not only convention; it also has underlying principles and a characteristic moral sensibility. He doesn't believe that there is a unique right path for tradition to take, but he knows that there are wrong paths – that is, paths that deviate from these principles and sensibilities. Indeed, the fact that there are objectively wrong paths in Jewish law is already assumed by the rabbis of the Mishna, who devote an entire tractate to the hypothetical situation in which the highest rabbinic court rules incorrectly.

Jewish tradition itself includes a mechanism for making such deviant paths unlikely: it mandates respect for, and hence emulation of, those with deep knowledge of and commitment to the principles and sensibilities embodied in tradition. The way this works in practice is that each one of us looks to our right and to our left and pays most attention to the practices of those who, as best as we can tell, have the best chance of getting it right. Of course, some people must be starting this cascade of emulation by acting independently. Among these, there are some (in Judaism, they typically are prominent rabbis) who are frequently emulated either directly or indirectly.

The upshot is this: the consensus that emerges gives weight to the practices of all those committed to tradition, but gives more weight to those who are recognized as authorities. It is crucial to note that the influence of these authorities is not a function of their position. Rather their position is a function of their influence.

Let's consider why this strategy makes sense – and, in particular, why it makes more sense than two alternative strategies: pure egalitarianism (in which everybody gets equal weight) and pure elitism (in which only experts get any weight at all).

Let's begin with a very crude version of the formal argument for egalitarianism. Suppose that – even after taking into account ignorance, stupidity, and self-serving bias – the average Joe has healthy enough instincts to give him a very slightly better than even chance of doing the right thing in some given situation. Next, suppose that many average Joes, acting independently of each other, "vote" through their actions in that situation. Given these assumptions, it can be proved[11] that whatever the majority does is almost certainly right.

The argument is crude – not necessarily wrong, but still crude – because the underlying assumptions generally don't hold: in real life, people don't act independently of each other. Moreover, there are whole strata of people who are plainly at least as likely to get it wrong as to get it right. In real life, mobs sometimes do really bad things.

So, let's make the more modest assumption that even those who are not bright lights when it comes to figuring out the right thing to do are at least fairly decent judges of character and have a reasonable chance of emulating the people with the best chance of getting things right. In this scenario, those who ultimately count the most will be those with the best chance of getting it right, while those unlikely to get it right will carry little weight.

Some versions of this "weighted-majority" strategy, which distributes influence broadly but not equally, have a higher probability of yielding the right answer than both egalitarianism, in which all opinions get equal weight, and pure elitism, in which only expert opinions count at all. In fact, under certain conditions, a particular version of the strategy is demonstrably optimal.[12]

---

11. The first proof was offered in Marquis de Condorcet, *Essai sur l'application de l'analyse à la probabilité des décisions rendues à la pluralité des voix* (1785). A more precise formulation of the necessary and sufficient conditions regarding voter competence for the result to hold is given in Daniel Berend and Jacob Paroush, "When Is Condorcet's Jury Theorem Valid?" *Social Choice and Welfare* 15, no. 4 (1998). For a popular presentation of some of these ideas see J. Surowiecki, *The Wisdom of Crowds* (New York: Anchor Books 2005).

12. S. Nitzan and J. Paroush, "Optimal Decision Rules in Uncertain Dichotomous Choice Situations," *International Economic Review* 23, no. 2 (1982): 289–97. For binary choice, the best method is one in which an independent voter with probability p of getting the right answer is given weight $\log(p/(1-p))$.

That's the simple argument for balancing egalitarianism with elitism. Here's a more sophisticated argument. If you're in England, you drive on the left side of the road; in most other places, you drive on the right. Either one of these options is fine, so long as everybody in any given place does the same thing. "Take your pick" is not a good option. This kind of thing is called a "coordination problem."

For example, there is no shortage of reasonable platforms for online social networks and most of us don't really care which one we use so long as our friends use the same one. Similarly, there's really no particular reason for a Hasid to prefer a high *shtreimel* (*spodek*) to a low *shtreimel*; all that matters is that he wear the same one as the Hasidim he eats kugel with. These things generally work themselves out. MySpace is history; Gerers wear high *shtreimlekh*. As soon as a coordination problem is resolved so that everybody is doing the same thing, it will not pay for any individual to buck the trend; in this sense, the process is said to have reached an equilibrium.

As is the case in the repeated Prisoner's Dilemma we considered above, coordination problems typically have multiple possible equilibria, some better than others. The reasons that we converge to one equilibrium rather than another are often mysterious, and we don't always end up in the best possible equilibrium.[13] And once we are settled in one, it's hard to escape it, even if it eventually proves to be bad for everybody. Imagine, for example, that some savvy startup offers a new social-network platform that is more transparent and less invasive than the current leading brand. Since nobody wants to be among the first million people to switch over, we are all trapped in a sub-optimal equilibrium. Not to compare, but for those on the dais at one of Stalin's speeches, applauding

---

13. On bad equilibria in coordination problems, see, for example, E. Yudkowsky, *Inadequate Equilibria: Where and How Civilizations Get Stuck* (Berkeley, CA: MIRI, 2017).

the great leader's bon mots was another kind of coordination trap; no one could afford to be the first to stop.[14]

Social norms, especially those tied up with signaling, are rife with sub-optimal equilibria. We have already seen why signals are necessary for facilitating cooperation, but there are many possible signals that could do the trick and we are likely sometimes to get stuck with ones we're not crazy about. *Shtreimlekh* can get bigger, hotter, and more expensive to the point where everybody feels a bit put upon. Bridge-burning signals, like not getting an education or a job, can also prove somewhat onerous. In all these cases, even if *everyone* would prefer a cheaper signal that would be good enough, who can afford to be the first to stop?

The answer is that someone with a great deal of prestige and clout can potentially catalyze an escape from a bad equilibrium. For example, the Gerer Rebbe can instruct his followers to buy only *shtreimlekh* made of artificial fur – or he can simply set an example himself. To generalize, a key, and usually under-appreciated, advantage of balancing egalitarianism with heavily weighted leadership is the increased chance of occasionally escaping a sub-optimal equilibrium in a coordination problem. To be sure, this works only if the leadership emerges through a process driven by popular demand, is sufficiently respectful of tradition to use its power judiciously, and is sufficiently salient or consensual to establish a new focal point around which a better equilibrium can coalesce.

Let's sum up. We have seen how it is advantageous for halakha to lie on a continuum between law and language: it preserves

---

14. A chilling story about this appears in Alexander Solzhenitsyn, *The Gulag Archipelago* (New York: Harper and Row, 1973), 69–70. This is an extreme example of what the economist Timur Kuran calls "preference falsification," in which people subject to social pressure publicly profess preferences or beliefs they don't actually hold. Massive preference falsification is subject to collapse when the revelation of true preferences by a few "dissidents" triggers a cascade. See T. Kuran, *Private Truths, Public Lies* (Cambridge, MA: Harvard University Press, 1997).

tradition, leverages both intuition and reason, and balances popular practice and rabbinic leadership. All of these are necessary. A community needs tradition to store wisdom, it needs moral intuition to set worthy goals and motivate us to pursue them, it needs reason to determine how to achieve goals efficiently and coherently, and it needs collective judgment to fine-tune tradition while overcoming individual bias.

But balancing intuition and reason, as well as egalitarianism and elitism, can be achieved only in the absence of a legislative body with power of enforcement. Let's now see why this point is crucial and, in particular, why halakha is viable precisely because its organizing unit is Shimen's community and not Heidi's state.

COMMUNITIES AND STATES

Shimen's attachment to community is not coincidental. All the fine properties of halakha considered above – robustness, adaptability, intuitiveness, and so forth – are possible precisely because halakha is a communal, rather than a governmental, process. As we have seen, communities don't legislate or enforce the way states do; one can escape from a community more easily than one can escape from a state; and, finally, communities are smaller than states and easily split into subcommunities. Each of these properties is essential for halakha to work.

With regard to legislation and enforcement, the matter is straightforward. Unlike legislation, which is a discrete event and is typically determined by a small group of legislators who are liable to have their own interests, social norms tend to be stable, adjusting gradually and in accordance with consensus. Furthermore, signaling, the importance of which we've discussed several times, is possible only when it is not enforced. If, for example, everybody were compelled by law to buy only kosher meat, buying kosher would fail as a signal – exactly as it fails when kosher meat is no more expensive or difficult to obtain than non-kosher meat. In such cases, we'd have to invent stringencies not required by law for the purpose of signaling piety. Thus, legislation and enforcement undercut key aspects of the way halakha works.

Furthermore, a community is defined by the social norms shared by its members, while a state's jurisdiction falls on all those who live in its territory. An individual who doesn't share a community's norms is *ipso facto* no longer part of that community; if a large enough sub-group develops different norms from the majority of the community, they become a distinct community in themselves. These two facts are crucial for the organic development of halakha. To see why, let's compare two types of organizations.

If you own a condo, you probably belong to some sort of homeowners' association. You might also be a member of one of your local synagogues. Both of these organizations provide useful services and charge fees, and both of them occasionally deal with contentious issues that engender squabbling, arm-twisting, and gossiping. But they're unlikely to occupy the same cell in your brain because the differences between them are so salient.

People who belong to a homeowners' association share a place of residence. That's it. They need to decide together when to paint the lobby and whose brother-in-law to hire to repair the roof. If someone doesn't like the color the board chose for the ceiling in the lobby, there's not much they can do about it short of selling the apartment in which they are heavily invested. If a whole group of people became disenchanted with the board's decisions, they could try to replace the board but they couldn't form a breakaway board. Neighbors in an apartment building don't necessarily have much in common that really matters, but they are stuck with each other and have no choice but to work out their differences regarding maintenance and such issues.

Members of a synagogue have a lot in common. They choose to pray a certain way, to observe Shabbat a certain way, and to assume a million unspoken truths about the right way to live. These shared norms and values define the synagogue. If someone doesn't share at least a fair portion of them, they would simply leave and pray elsewhere or nowhere. If a whole group of people became disenchanted with the synagogue's policies, they could try to form a breakaway synagogue with policies that reflect their own preferences.

Halakha remains substantive and adapts slowly and steadily precisely because, like a synagogue but unlike a home-owners' association, those who don't share its underlying principles cease by mutual consent to be voting members (though I acknowledge that leaving a tight-knit community is often painful and difficult).

There is yet another subtle way in which the communal basis of halakha contributes to its viability. Consider the development of distinct subcommunities created by fissures. When one looks too closely at fissures that split highly observant communities – whether they be succession battles in the Ponevezh yeshiva in Israel or similar struggles in the hasidic communities of Bobov and Satmar in New York – it might appear as if all that is at stake is ego and money. But this is an illusion; it is merely the outer shell of a deeper phenomenon.

When communities exceed a certain size and inter-personal relationships within the community become overly thin, the urge to seek grounds for splitting becomes irresistible. The short-term results are not always aesthetically pleasing, but such splits result in more tight-knit and homogeneous communities, each of which takes advantage of local knowledge and is adapted to its situation.

Moreover, when people become more aware of the variety of extant community traditions, such as happens during mass migrations, the multiplicity of communities has the ironic consequence of highlighting the common core of halakha that is common to all these diverse communities. Finally, subcommunities that prove to be poorly adapted, usually because the barriers between them and non-halakhic cultures are too low, simply cease to exist, while those that are well adapted thrive and grow in influence. This too leads to better-adapted communities.

Of course, things can go badly wrong when we forget the difference between synagogues and homeowners' associations or, more broadly, between religious communities and states. In Part 4, we'll consider the problems that ensue when religious communities seek to exploit the coercive power of the state to enforce their preferred social norms. But now let's return to our friend Heidi, who, oddly enough, wishes to do just that.

Chapter 8

The Perils of Social Engineering

Shimen identifies strongly with his community and much less with the country in which he happens to live, but he understands perfectly well that the state serves many important functions that could not be served by his community. Shimen and his friends are aware that halakha has little to say about contemporary public policy and that it lacks the sometimes-necessary strong hand of the state. They are also grateful for the freedom and security afforded them by the United States and by the cultural openness so central to the American ethos. So Shimen's community has settled upon a pragmatic balance between the roles it reserves for itself and those it leaves to the state.

Like Shimen, Heidi has friends and neighbors who constitute a community of sorts for her. She shares with her community values and attitudes, as well as social norms and even rituals and signaling conventions. But Heidi's community has not had the long arc of tradition required to develop a system of social norms as rich and detailed as that of Shimen's community. Nor does it have the well-developed communal institutions required to promote the degree of interdependence, voluntary compliance, and social capital characteristic of Shimen's community. For lack of a better alternative, Heidi uses the state to fill the gap. There are a considerable number of matters, mostly involving regulation and redistribution, that Shimen's community manages for itself with as little state interference as possible, but that Heidi regards as central roles of the state.

To be sure, it is not the case that the state serves as the focal point of Heidi's tribal devotion in the way that Shimen's community does for him. Rather, her lack of a community that could serve as an alternative to the state inclines Heidi to turn to the state by default. As we will see, in many cases the state is the wrong venue for achieving Heidi's goals. Moreover, Heidi's rejection of Shimen's pragmatic balance between communal norms and state laws and between popular tradition and expert-designed policy does not lead, as she imagines, to a different but better balance. Rather, as we saw above in the case of moral foundations, Heidi's approach simply fails to find a stable balance between community and state and instead swings between extremes in a way that undermines her own objectives.

HEIDI READS RAWLS

Let's consider Heidi's position on the proper roles of the state. Heidi wants the state to legislate and enforce policies that promote public welfare and equality. She supports, among other things, state-enforced redistribution of income, environmental regulation, safety regulation, minimum-wage laws, rent control, and anti-discrimination laws. But, at the same time, she strongly opposes any state involvement in the enforcement of the two flavors of morality other than fairness, the ones involving restraint and loyalty. She wishes, for example, to liberalize abortion laws (wherever they still exist) and euthanasia laws and to eliminate any residual legal barriers to recognizing same-sex marriages. She wants state-funded schools to refrain from inculcating what she regards as jingoistic or religious values.

There are several grounds for Heidi's preferences. To begin with, as we have seen, the kind of morality that is important to Heidi is, to a large extent, subsumed by public welfare and equality. But if pressed to justify her support for state involvement in welfare but not in the flavors of morality not associated with welfare, Heidi would probably appeal to the "veil of ignorance" argument of the late political philosopher John Rawls.[1]

Rawls's famous thought experiment asks us to imagine that we are a group of people wishing to agree upon certain principles according to which we will organize our society. So far this is the usual "social contract" idea. The wrinkle is that you, like everyone else in the game, know nothing about yourself: neither your age nor your sex, neither your skills nor your income potential, nor your religion, your beliefs or commitments, or your social, business, or other affiliations. Nothing.

Assuming we are rational actors, what principles would we agree on? Rawls argues that we'd all agree that each person should have the maximum degree of liberty consistent with others having that same degree of liberty. In particular, since we don't know anything about our prior moral affiliations and commitments, we'd all agree that the state should not impose any particular community's definition of what constitutes morality. In fact, "comprehensive doctrines" – Rawls's fancy way of referring to religion – are to be banned from public discourse as grounds for promoting policy.

The second principle that we'd all agree on is that, given some set of possible distributions of goods, we should choose the specific distribution that gives the most to the poorest member of

1. John Rawls, *A Theory of Justice* (Cambridge, MA: Belknap Press, 1971).

society (an arrangement to which you'd agree because that poorest member might be you). This, in very broad strokes, is the argument for including within the state's purview some version of equality and, more broadly, public welfare.

In short, then, welfare and equality are public business, but other flavors of morality and the cultivation of virtue are private business. This is a conclusion that Heidi accepts wholeheartedly. Shimen, on the other hand, is of the view that both welfare and virtue should be handled, to a large extent, by communities.

But there's a weird anomaly in Heidi's position. Since Heidi wants the state out of the business of promoting virtue, we might expect her to enthusiastically approve of voluntary moral communities like Shimen's. After all, Rawls presumably wants the state out of the morality business precisely so that religious communities like Shimen's can flourish without state interference. Yet Heidi disapproves of Shimen's community, and others of the same type, for oppressing individuals and undercutting the state. What's up with that?

Teasing out the assumptions that underlie Rawls's thought experiment gives away the game. How would I wish to organize society after I have peeled away my affiliations, loyalties, and beliefs, and everything else that makes me *me*? The question hardly seems coherent since, at that stage, who exactly would be left with interests to negotiate? Rawls and Heidi simply assume that there is some "unencumbered self," as political philosopher Michael Sandel puts it,[2] independent of and prior to the affiliations that constitute my identity, and that we can somehow imagine the preferences of these unencumbered selves as they organize themselves politically. But, in fact, we only have preferences at all because we are encumbered.

---

2. M. Sandel, *Liberalism and the Limits of Justice* (Cambridge, UK: Cambridge University Press, 1998).

Rawls's thought experiment resonates more with Heidi than it does with Shimen; it seems that in real life Shimen and Heidi are not equally encumbered. Shimen's life is defined by his identification with a specific people committed to the perpetuation and development of a specific culture. Shimen knows what it feels like to have nothing, so he doesn't underestimate the importance of material goods, but these goods don't have symbolic value for him; what he really wants is the meaning and purpose that he gets from participating in the ongoing project of the Jews. What would Shimen want if he were not a Jew? Not a meaningful question.

For Heidi, on the other hand, banning "comprehensive doctrines" from public discourse doesn't cost a thing. While Shimen wants freedom *to* participate in a specific communal project that connects the past with the future and that gives his life meaning and purpose, Heidi wants freedom *from* such projects. Heidi's aspiration for freedom for herself and for others is understandable, but struggling for freedom *from* without also struggling for freedom *to* generates a lot of negative energy.

Instead of giving moral communities space to flourish, as the Rawlsian model would seem to suggest, Heidi does subtle combat with these communities. In the name of liberty, she seeks to clip their wings so that the flavors of morality that are less meaningful to her devolve to individuals. And, in the name of public welfare, she seeks to crowd out moral communities by having the state take over the roles traditionally played by such communities.

Heidi's battle against moral communities gets to march under the high-minded banners of liberty and public welfare, but constitutes thin gruel to build a life around. In the end, a culture built on resentment of others' moral traditions can arouse, but it can't fulfill.

WHAT IS SEEN AND WHAT IS NOT SEEN

High-minded banners aside, one thing that the extension of state power at the expense of communities rarely achieves is the advancement of either public welfare or liberty. States lack the adaptive qualities of communities that we discussed above. Weakening the soft authority of communities in favor of the hard power of states is likely both to weaken welfare and to diminish liberty.

As we have seen, Heidi holds two views: first, she argues in favor of state intervention in the functioning of markets for the purpose of advancing what she regards as public welfare, and, second, she argues against state involvement in promoting virtue. But any advocate of freedom for individuals and communities ought to lament that she is too sincere about the former and insufficiently sincere about the latter.

Let's start with the costs of the kind of state intervention in markets that Heidi favors and then proceed to the insincerity of Heidi's ostensible opposition to state promotion of virtue.

I'm an advocate of liberty, but I'm no anarchist. Let's agree that certain functions are most efficiently handled by the state: providing security against crime and external threats, enforcing contracts and compensation for damages, and ensuring the supply of certain public goods that the market might otherwise fail to produce efficiently. But Heidi's preferences for state intervention go well beyond these instances. Some of the roles Heidi is happy for the state to play are superfluous and harmful since markets would do fine without them; others are just better left to civil society.

For example, Heidi likes regulation, especially the kind that appears to protect the weak from the predations of the powerful. Minimum-wage laws, affirmative action, consumer-protection laws, occupational licensure, rent control, it's all good.[3] What, after all, could be bad about looking out for the modest laborer, the innocent consumer, and the oppressed minority? As it turns

---

3. On the ideological roots of the progressive fondness for regulation, see T. Sowell, *The Vision of the Anointed* (New York: Basic Books, 1995).

out, however, the attractiveness of these sorts of regulations relies on a sleight of hand: their benefits are more easily seen than their costs.[4]

The benefits of minimum-wage laws for those who would otherwise earn less are more conspicuous than the harm to those whom such laws cause to remain, or become, unemployed and to the companies that close, or never open, due to higher labor costs. The benefit of affirmative action for the less-qualified minority worker who is hired is more evident than the harm caused to the qualified worker who is not hired, to the qualified minority worker who is wrongly presumed to have been given a break, and to the shareholders and customers of the company that must manage with a sub-optimal labor force. The benefits that accrue to consumers from additional regulation on businesses are more visible than the costs those same consumers will incur when the increased expense of doing business is passed on to them and when potential competitors are deterred from entering the market by onerous compliance costs.

Occupational licensure is a particularly instructive example. The power the state gives to professional guilds to create entry barriers to a profession are ostensibly designed to protect consumers. But somehow, it's never consumers who clamor for such barriers, but rather those already in the profession. Note, for example, that only taxi drivers are convinced that Uber drivers are potential kidnappers of passengers; Uber passengers themselves seem blithely unconcerned. The competition that would result from lower barriers to entry into a profession challenges those already in the guild but benefits consumers, as it lowers prices and increases the availability and accessibility of the provided service.

---

4. Frederic Bastiat, *That Which Is Seen, and That Which Is Not Seen* (1850). Accessible at http://bastiat.org/en/twisatwins.html.

Why, then, do politicians so often favor the kind of regulation that keeps barriers high? The answer is "concentrated benefits, dispersed costs": that is, the benefits of such regulation to licensed cosmetologists, barbers, undertakers, and what-have-you are worth enough to these professionals to finance political pressure, but the costs of that regulation to somebody with fingernails, hair, or deceased relatives will never be high enough to get them to march on the Capitol.[5]

Sometimes the costs of state regulation are not just unseen but unanticipated. Like other Manhattanites who don't own real estate, Heidi is fond of rent control. Are we seriously going to allow some rapacious landlord to take 7,000 bucks a month for that tiny apartment? A reasonable cap on rent would level the playing field and couldn't possibly do anyone any harm, right?

Well, this has been tried in dozens of cities. How does it play out? Since the price is held below the natural market price, the supply goes down as landlords take apartments off the market and builders postpone building projects. As the supply of rent-controlled apartments goes down, the prices of non-controlled apartments go up. Since rents are fixed, landlords have no financial incentive to raise the values of their properties, so they neglect them. Alice would like to move out of her apartment but fears she won't find another one that is rent-controlled, so she's locked into a sub-optimal situation, which locks out Bob, who'd prefer to move into Alice's apartment – and so on. Given the diminished supply of available apartments along with artificially low prices, potential tenants compete for available apartments; landlords, who would ordinarily rent to the highest bidder, now must choose among them arbitrarily. Often a landlord will simply prefer the ones whose racial or ethnic profile or family structure makes him most

---

5. Mancur Olson, *The Logic of Collective Action: Public Goods and the Theory of Groups* (Cambridge, MA: Harvard University Press, 1965).

comfortable. Of course, a landlord might also prefer the potential tenant who offers to make side payments under the table above the maximum rent allowed by law. The authorities, cottoning on to this, will send inspectors to catch such scofflaws and will encourage snitching and lawsuits; landlords will bribe inspectors to look the other way.

What's the upshot? Heidi's innocent plan for creating affordable housing has indeed lowered rents for some people, but at the cost of higher rents for other people, shortages, lock-ins, slums, discrimination, under-the-table dealing, ratting, litigation, and bribery. Overall, not a good deal.

Now let's move from markets to civil society and consider two important examples where civil society can potentially solve problems better than states can. Let's start with the lake that we considered in Part 1. Recall that the situation was such that if everybody fishes a bit too much the lake will be depleted of fish. This is an example of the problem of "the commons": that is, resources like fishing sites, grazing pastures, and water reservoirs that are easily accessible to some community of potential users but subject to short-term overuse that results in long-term damage to all the users.[6] The theory is that, because cheating pays, agreements among players not to overuse the resource can't hold without state enforcement. Thus, we might want the state involved in legislating limitations on exploitation of such resources.

In our discussion of the repeated Prisoner's Dilemma in Part 1, we found that cooperation is possible in the long run if players can successfully signal each other that they have low discount rates. The problem of the commons is simply an example of a repeated Prisoner's Dilemma with many players, so that cooperation can develop under analogous circumstances. So, in principle,

---

6. G. Hardin, "The Tragedy of the Commons," *Science* 162, issue 3859 (1968): 1243–48.

participants should be able to cooperate and self-police without state intervention, provided they develop trust based on shared social norms.

In fact, this is borne out in real life. The political economist Elinor Ostrom[7] found many examples of communities successfully sharing pooled resources, including Swiss farming villages sharing grazing meadows and Turkish fishermen sharing fishing sites. Among the key features of successful self-policing communities such as these are clear markers of community membership, and rules that are established by the members themselves without state interference and that reflect shared social norms. Such solutions tend to develop bottom up over long periods, respecting time-tested traditions.

I'm not suggesting that all common-pool resources can be self-administered by communities, but merely that, contrary to Heidi's assumption, state intervention is not always necessary or even helpful. States are too centralized to permit local solutions, too populous to allow direct involvement of citizens in making rules, too heterogeneous to develop the necessary degree of trust, and too dependent on experts to honor time-tested norms. As we saw in the previous chapter, respected leaders acting from within communal traditions in an unofficial capacity are capable of catalyzing a shift from a sub-optimal equilibrium to a better one, in a way that states often cannot. But it's also true that states have the advantage of raw coercive power and sometimes that does the trick.

Now consider another example of state overreach in communal affairs: redistribution and entitlements. Shimen's community takes care of its own. When the need arises, a loan or gift is discreetly arranged for a community member fallen on hard times.

---

7. Elinor Ostrom, *Governing the Commons: The Evolution of Institutions for Collective Action (Political Economy of Institutions and Decisions)* (Cambridge, UK: Cambridge University Press, 1990).

In addition, there is a communal fund administered by trusted members of the community who are generally personally familiar with both donors and recipients. They can establish criteria of eligibility that don't encourage those who could be self-reliant to become dependent on handouts. Charity within Shimen's community is regarded by both donors and recipients as a form of good fellowship that might in the future be flowing in the reverse direction. It strengthens communal bonds and increases aggregate social capital.

Heidi will counter correctly that communal funds are narrow in scope, that some people don't belong to any such community, and that some communities lack the resources to take care of their own. Entitlements administered by the state out of taxpayer money reach everyone qualified to receive them, regardless of community affiliation. Moreover, they are distributed according to transparent and objective criteria. In addition, states have tools for coordinating and tracking disbursements to avoid duplication and waste, as well as enforcement mechanisms to punish and deter fraud.

All that is true and explains why the safety net provided by the state cannot be dismantled altogether. Nevertheless, there are social costs of government handouts. Unlike communal charities, state entitlements are distributed by bureaucrats with limited incentive to execute their jobs in an efficient manner. These bureaucracies are liable to become bloated and unresponsive to the faceless masses seeking their aid. Furthermore, bureaucracies are committed to rigid rules that are easily gamed, thus giving maximal rewards to cheaters and free riders. Often, even perfectly honest people who would otherwise seek gainful employment are disincentivized from doing so by the prospect of easy money. As massive research has shown, the welfare state undermines self-reliance and, even more, our very appreciation of the value of self-reliance.

Most of all, the welfare state diminishes social capital. By encouraging reliance on entitlements for economic security, the welfare state undoes the bonds of dependence within families and communities. To Heidi, this is a feature and not a bug. But here is where she misses the main point. As many lonely people discover far too late, the reliance of children on their parents and, subsequently, of parents on their children, and the reliance of members of communities on each other, are what fill our lives with meaning, our social bonds with substance and warmth, and our futures with hope.

Sadly, the bureaucratic regulatory welfare state has been so successful at destroying families and communities that it has rendered itself necessary.

BOOTLEGGERS AND BAPTISTS

Heidi lacks a community that provides social welfare and moral guidance in the substantive and detailed way that Shimen's community supplies these things for him. Instead, she demands that the state provide social welfare and that morality not subsumed under welfare be left to individuals' discretion. In this way, she expects to advance equality (through state welfare) and freedom (through respect for individual discretion in moral matters).

Both these objectives are honorable, but Heidi doesn't actually achieve either one of them. With regard to social welfare, the state can sometimes be useful, but, as we have seen, it is in most cases less effective than communities at advancing social welfare. With regard to freedom, Heidi's approach fails in two different ways: first, as I'll explain in what follows, her defense of individual freedom is somewhat inconsistent; second, in those instances in which Heidi is sincere about freedom, she undermines the basis for her own society's survival.

Shimen and Heidi agree that it is risky to get the state involved in moral matters. Neither one does so from behind the

Rawlsian veil of ignorance; each simply fears the power of the state being brought to bear on somebody else's side of some moral issue. For Shimen, the moral slack is taken up by his community, but for Heidi, not so much.

Like everyone else, Heidi is instinctively revolted by bad behavior. Her moral indignation can't simply be repressed; it needs an outlet. Heidi deals with these annoyingly insistent instincts by expanding the scope of welfare sufficiently to give cover to policies designed to address her instinctive contempt for moral transgressions. She ignores the costs that accompany laws regarding recycling, smoking, trans fats, super-sized sodas, rent control, discrimination, and the like. In fact, she is pleased to see contamination, greed, gluttony, and disrespect punished. This is righteous indignation invoking the power of the state, masquerading as a concern for social welfare.

Restrictions on the sale of alcohol are sometimes attributed to the unwitting cooperation of "bootleggers and Baptists." This shorthand, popularized by the economist Bruce Yandle,[8] neatly captures the broader principle that some regulation passes because it simultaneously serves the interests of "bootleggers," who expect to profit from it, and "Baptists," whose moral indignation it gratifies. Nowadays, Heidi is much more likely to be the Baptist than is Shimen.

Recall that Heidi resents the influence wielded by rabbis in Jewish communities like Shimen's or that of her parents. But to put some perspective on the matter, we might compare the most influential halakhic authority in New York (whoever he is) with, say, the New York City Commissioner of Health, of whose regulatory powers Heidi approves. The commissioner can ban the sale of artificial trans fats if she decides they're bad for you; the rabbi can ban them only if he can provide a persuasive halakhic basis for doing so. The commissioner can be fired only by the mayor;

---

8. Adam Smith and Bruce Yandle, *Bootleggers and Baptists: How Economic Forces and Moral Persuasion Interact to Shape Regulatory Politics* (Washington, DC: Cato Institute, 2014).

the rabbi can simply be abandoned by his followers. The commissioner can have you fined or imprisoned if you violate the ban; the rabbi can stop eating in your house.

In short, loosening the grip of communal norms merely tightens the grip of state regulation; thus, it is more likely to diminish liberty than to promote it. In the timeless words of Alexis de Tocqueville:

> After having thus taken each individual one by one into its powerful hands, and having molded him as it pleases, the sovereign power extends its arms over the entire society; it covers the surface of society with a network of small, complicated, minute, and uniform rules, which the most original minds and the most vigorous souls cannot break through to go beyond the crowd; it does not break wills, but it softens them, bends them and directs them; it rarely forces action, but it constantly opposes your acting; it does not destroy, it prevents birth; it does not tyrannize, it hinders, it represses, it enervates, it extinguishes, it stupefies, and finally it reduces each nation to being nothing more than a flock of timid and industrious animals, of which the government is the shepherd.[9]

Heidi's approach to the relative powers of communities and states also undermines the cause of fairness. The way Heidi sees the world, Shimen and others in communities like Shimen's are beholden to "comprehensive doctrines," while Heidi's views on public affairs are simply neutral.[10] But, this notion of a neutral

---

9. Alexis de Tocqueville, *Democracy in America*, vol. 2, 4:6 (1840).

10. The artificiality of this supposed neutrality is explored at length in, for example, Alasdair MacIntyre, *Whose Justice? Which Rationality?* (South Bend, IN: Notre Dame University Press, 1988); Robert P. George, *Clash of Orthodoxies* (Wilmington, DE: ISI Press, 2001); Steven D. Smith, *The Disenchantment of Secular Discourse* (Cambridge, MA: Harvard University Press, 2010).

culture makes as much sense as the notion of speaking language without speaking a specific language.[11] Or, as the philosopher Sidney Morgenbesser facetiously answered when asked by a waiter if he wanted potato soup, vegetable soup, or chicken soup, "None of those, just plain soup."

Heidi's defense of a neutral public culture is simply cosmopolitan tribalism. This tribalism might be dismissed as mildly amusing if not for the fact that Heidi insists that, as a shared neutral space, the public square must reflect her "neutral" views. In particular, public education and publicly funded culture must be free of even the most benign expressions of religion and patriotism or the encouragement of virtues associated with these dangerous doctrines, like temperance, fortitude, gratitude, or prudence.

Heidi places great burdens on the state, yet she favors a culture that doesn't develop the very qualities of character needed to keep a republic. A public square and an education system that systematically undermine the virtues required to sustain a society will, unsurprisingly, produce a generation of citizens who lack those virtues.

For example, Heidi's radical daughter, Amber.

AMBER'S PURITANISM

Heidi lives by rules, but she could never quite bring herself to impose rules on Amber. Heidi emphasized to the young Amber the importance of fairness, but such fairness was never reduced to the kinds of specific rules that societies evolve to give fairness concrete definition. Instead, Amber learned to recognize *un*fairness mainly by the feelings of outrage that welled up inside her from time to time. When Heidi would instruct young Amber to

---

11. See also George Santayana, *The Life of Reason: Reason in Religion* (New York: Charles Scribner, 1905), chapter 1: "The attempt to speak without speaking any particular language is not more hopeless than the attempt to have a religion that shall be no religion in particular."

"question authority," as she often did, Amber heard only "trust your own feelings." And, to this day, nothing arouses Amber's sense of outrage more than having her feelings – or her opinions, which for her are interchangeable with her feelings – challenged.[12]

Amber's political views reflect her upbringing and bring into sharp relief the subtle cracks in Heidi's political views. Heidi's lack of a true community, and lack of appreciation for the benefits of such communities, has led her to assign liberty only to individuals and authority only to states. This is self-undermining, as we have seen, but at least individual liberty and state authority are, within reasonable limits, worth pursuing. Amber has simply abandoned both of these as objectives.

Heidi wishes to centralize power by shifting the functions of traditional communities to the state. This is, as we have seen, often inefficient or overbearing, but at least it allows citizens of the state to collectively express whatever common ethos they share. But Amber, taking her own liberty and prosperity for granted, sees only the flaws in the American ethos; the United States, like every other successful democracy, is, as far as Amber is concerned, racist, colonialist, materialistic, and altogether oppressive. Her contempt for these countries is so great that she wishes to centralize power even more than Heidi does, by shifting the functions of states to transnational organizations like the EU and the UN. Such organizations inevitably cater to the rather thin common denominator of their constituents; often this seems to be limited to the love of stifling bureaucracy and the fear and loathing of Jewish power. Amber's version of globalism thus exaggerates the worst aspects of Heidi's reliance on the state, while eliminating the positive aspects of Heidi's residual allegiance to her country.

---

12. Greg Lukianoff and Jonathan Haidt, *The Coddling of the American Mind: How Good Intentions and Bad Ideas Are Setting Up a Generation for Failure* (New York: Penguin Books, 2018).

Heidi indulges her righteous indignation by supporting overly aggressive regulation, but she is at least aware that this can rub up against individual liberty. Amber's righteous indignation is downright puritanical and leaves almost no room at all for individual liberty. She wishes to criminalize and prosecute male lust and boorishness, including non-coercive sexual advances once regarded as benign, and any behavior that threatens her self-esteem. In cases of alleged sexual misconduct on campus she is an advocate of disciplinary tribunals that don't pretend to respect due process or impartiality.

If, in the name of inclusiveness, Heidi wishes to keep religious expression out of the public square, Amber wishes to criminalize some such expression. In her view, we ought to consider shutting down religious institutions that don't accommodate same-sex marriages, delicensing doctors who won't perform abortions, and silencing public speakers who suggest that human nature isn't infinitely malleable. Amber has replaced the free exchange of views with "cancel culture," and national allegiance with cosmocratic imperialism.

In short, then, the abandonment of cohesive religious communities like Shimen's is less likely to be leading us to a secular paradise of freedom and equality than to a dystopic world in which transnational secular elites prosecute "sin" and persecute religion.

* * *

The key takeaway of Part 2 is that for a system of social norms to be adaptive it must develop through a process that combines respect for tradition, aggregation of the moral intuitions of the committed, and expert reasoning. Such a combination is possible for communities of like-minded people, like Shimen's, but is not possible in societies that depend primarily on laws that are legislated and enforced from the top down.

The arguments presented here are somewhat preliminary, but they suggest that exploration of the mechanisms through which tradition, intuition aggregation, and expert reasoning might interact optimally in a given society could serve as an organizing principle for a fruitful research program.

To a large extent, though, the appropriate balance depends on the beliefs of that society about its cultural heritage and its destiny and purposes. This is the topic of Part 3.

PART 3

What Is the Connection Between Belief and Commitment?

In this part of the book, we'll consider the relationship between religious belief and a commitment to a particular system of social norms. We'll confront Heidi's charge that Shimen's whole way of life is predicated on beliefs that are unscientific and ahistorical. We'll address a number of questions in confronting this objection: Which is prior for Shimen, belief or commitment? Is one possible without the other? What is the actual foundation upon which anyone's beliefs rest?

Chapter 9

Jewish Belief and Its Critics

In the first two parts of this book, I have focused on the differences between Shimen's and Heidi's respective practices. One plausible-sounding objection to my approach is that I should be talking about their beliefs, not their lifestyles. After all, aren't the disagreements between Shimen and Heidi about how to live merely second-order differences that follow inevitably from their irreconcilable beliefs about nature, history, and theology?

Well, if you insist, we can talk about these irreconcilable differences of belief. But, I must tell you right up front that the answer to your semi-rhetorical question is *no*. Young Shimen didn't contemplate nature and history and conclude, like our Father Abraham, that there must be a "ruler of the castle."[1] He was raised to honor particular virtues and traditions long before he had the most rudimentary ability to contemplate the stuff of belief. And among the traditions that he honors is the affirmation of certain claims about the world.

---

1. Bereshit Rabba 39:1.

Simply put, the direction of the causality implicit in the question above is exactly backward: in fact, virtues and traditions are primary and beliefs are derivative. This raises lots of obvious questions (how can we choose to believe something?), all of which we'll get to soon enough. For now, I want briefly to outline, in a perfectly naive way, traditional Jewish beliefs about the world. Later, we'll take a deeper dive and reconsider both the content and nature of traditional Jewish belief, but at this stage let's all just get on the same page that Shimen was on as a boy in *ḥeder* (religious elementary school) in Poland long before The War.

ḤEDER BELIEF

God created the universe, including the laws of nature. These laws hold most of the time but can be broken when God sees fit to intercede in the course of events by performing miracles. God revealed Himself to the forefathers of the Jewish people, promising that their descendants would be plentiful, would face special challenges, and would reap special rewards.

Our ancestors, the chosen descendants of these forefathers, were enslaved in Egypt and redeemed by God's hand amidst many miracles. The proto-nation redeemed from Egypt received the Torah in the desert at Sinai, through the agency of Moses, the greatest of all prophets. The received Torah consisted of the Written Torah, dictated by God to Moses in the precise words of the Five Books of Moses that we have today, along with an accompanying Oral Law that served as the basis of interpretation of the Torah. With God's direct help, the nascent nation conquered the Land of Israel, as had been promised to its forefathers, established the Davidic line of kings, and built the Temple in Jerusalem. But then, in retribution for various sins, the First Temple, and eventually the Second Temple, were destroyed, and the Jews were banished to the four corners of the earth.

The Written Torah and the Oral Law, as faithfully transmitted from Sinai and further interpreted by rabbis over all subsequent generations, are binding on all Jews. The law unfolds over generations through a guided process that accurately reveals its original intent: leading rabbis of each generation are divinely inspired, and the Jews as a nation possess the collective intuition of the "children of prophets,"[2] though in diminishing degrees with the passage of time.

The Jews are rewarded and punished, collectively and individually, in accordance with their observance of God's laws. Those who, for some reason, do not get their just deserts in this world are compensated or called to task in another world, obscure to us. One day, when they merit it, the Jews will be redeemed by God through the hand of the Messiah and returned to the Land of Israel, where they will rebuild the Temple and live harmoniously according to God's law. They will be ruled once again by kings from the line of David and by the renewed Sanhedrin, and will be free of the yoke of foreign nations. Ultimately, some of the dead will be resurrected and will share in this idyllic existence.

That, in a nutshell, is what Shimen – and every other *ḥeder* student in the past millennium – received as the basic truths of Judaism. Some of those *ḥeder* students went happily through life believing exactly that in a perfectly literal way. But others, including many who remained faithful to the tradition, found it more congenial, as their intellectual lives matured, to distinguish the essence of these beliefs from secondary elements or to interpret some aspects of this narrative in a more abstract form than the one they had received in *ḥeder*.

If you are of the former type, you probably ought to skip straight to Part 4.[3] For those in the latter camp, let's confront Heidi's serious objections to the *ḥeder* version of Jewish belief.

---

2. Pesaḥim 66a.
3. See Maimonides, *Mishneh Torah, Hilkhot Avoda Zara* [Laws of Idolatry] 2:3.

HEIDI'S SKEPTICISM

Heidi is proud to be a rational person; she is committed to accepting only what follows from evidence and reason. In her view, this criterion is not met by any of the traditional Jewish beliefs I've just enumerated. She notes with no small amount of disdain that Shimen and those like him seem never to have critically contemplated any of their beliefs in the light of readily available scientific and historical facts.

Heidi strives to be objective, to believe only what an unbiased person would believe. In her view, such a person would not place Jews at the center of the cosmos. Many tribes imagine that the world revolves around their own petty comings and goings, and they are all obviously wrong. The Jews are just another such tribe. From an objective point of view, their myths about their own chosenness are delusional, if not dangerous.

If she bothers engaging with specific canonical Jewish beliefs at all, she doesn't find much of value. It isn't so much that these beliefs are demonstrably false as that they are farfetched and there is no particular reason to believe them.

As far as Heidi can tell, modern cosmology, geology, and astronomy yield immeasurably more insight into the formation of heaven and earth than does the biblical narrative, and so does the theory of evolution concerning the origins of plant and animal life. She's not quite sure what it means for God to have created these things – and she's pretty sure Shimen doesn't, either – but she's reasonably confident that it doesn't add much to the picture that scientists have painted.

The probability that Heidi intuitively assigns to *any* book having been written by God is vanishingly low, and there isn't much in the Torah's inconsistent patchwork of dubious legends and rituals that screams out to Heidi that she needs to revise her assessment with regard to this particular book.

Reports of miracles, in the Torah and elsewhere, are more plausibly explained as the products of imagination or deception than as actual breaches of the laws of nature. All modern tales of miracles with which Heidi is familiar are either the products of wishful thinking on the part of religious enthusiasts or misinterpretations of random events. Somebody has to win the lottery, but to the lucky winner it always looks like a miracle.

Heidi is also not persuaded by claims that rabbis, ancient or modern, are divinely inspired. Some of them are indeed unusually clever, but she finds it hard to fathom how men in direct contact with the Holy Spirit could be so wrong about so many things. The rabbis seem to live in a parallel universe in which insects are spontaneously generated from inorganic material, human and animal anatomies do not resemble any form recognizable to moderns, the earth is flat, the sun circles back behind an opaque sky at night, and provable theorems of geometry and trigonometry are false.

Nothing in Heidi's experience suggests that the good are rewarded and the wicked are punished; as often as not, the opposite seems to be the case. The invention of an invisible world where things are evened out is an embarrassingly artificial rationalization that only highlights the salience of the problem.

The claim of chosenness and the belief that the entire course of human history is directed toward Jewish political redemption strike Heidi as nothing less than a form of national narcissism. As for resurrection, she has no clue what to make of it. If she were to be resurrected (in what form? at what age? with which memories and emotions preserved?), she could hardly imagine what connection her resurrected self would have with her present self and why she should care.

In short, for Heidi the whole package of canonical Jewish beliefs does not hold the slightest credibility or appeal.

Heidi's attacks are substantial and present us with a formidable challenge. I won't make the slightest attempt to refute them directly. Rather, I'll consider whether it is actually possible for Heidi, or anyone else, to believe "only what follows from evidence and reason" or "only what an unbiased person would believe." Heidi's presumptions on this score are rooted in a misunderstanding of the nature of belief.

First, however, we need to consider the true substance and nature of the adult Shimen's beliefs.

Chapter 10

Beyond Naivete

Like any rational person, Shimen draws conclusions about the workings of nature, including human nature, from his own experience and from the reported experience of others. Nevertheless, Shimen differs from Heidi in that he does not presume to construct all his beliefs about the world on the basis of evidence alone. In particular, we shall see that Shimen's most fundamental religious beliefs can be defined only subsequent to and in light of his prior commitment to Judaism.

Let's begin by organizing the canonical Jewish narrative we laid out above into elaborations of three principles: that the Torah was revealed to the Jewish people by God; that those who follow the Torah will be rewarded; and that Jewish history is directed toward messianic redemption. The rest of the narrative consists of amplifications and embellishments of these principles. Thus, the narrative of events leading to the Jews standing at Sinai gives context to the revelation of God's will to a specific nation. Miracles performed at various historical junctures demonstrate God's ability and determination to reward the righteous and punish the wicked. The rise and fall of the Davidic dynasty and of the First and Second Temples and the implied trajectory of subsequent Jewish history set the stage for future redemption.

Now let's get to the crux of these three principles. Each of the three is an aspect of the *single* belief that Judaism is a directed process linking the Jewish past with the Jewish future. The aspects of this single claim are that (a) the process developed organically from some non-arbitrary point ("revelation"); (b) the process is headed toward some non-arbitrary point ("redemption"); and (c) participation (and non-participation) in the process is self-reinforcing ("reward and punishment"). The rest is commentary.

As an empirical matter, different people understand these principles at different levels of abstraction. That's because there is a tradeoff here between gripping the soul with the narrative power of concrete beliefs and gripping the intellect with the plausibility of abstract beliefs. For some, it may be enough to believe that Judaism developed helter-skelter from some special origins in the murky past, but others might need the conviction that every detail of Judaism such as it is today can be traced directly to an original revelation in a specific place at a specific time.

For some, it may be enough that the process is limping forward in some vaguely understood positive direction, but others might need the ultimate destination of the process to be specified in terms of concrete political events and miraculous interventions, and for signs of the imminence and inevitability of such events to be already discernible.

For some, the satisfaction of leading a life bound to Torah is its own reward, but others might need to be assured that the righteous reap rewards and the wicked suffer punishments in the most prosaic of ways, preferably instantly and in plain sight.

Each person strikes the balance that works for him or her. In short, if we were to characterize actual Jewish belief such as it appears in the wild, we would find that different people codify it at different degrees of abstraction.

The key point for this stage of my argument is that the subject matter of Jewish belief is Jewish practice. The principles of Jewish belief, as we formulated them, are *about* the unfolding of Jewish tradition and the destiny of the people committed to that tradition, so that Jewish belief is empty without some prior definition of Jewish practice.[1] This point becomes much sharper when we consider not the content of belief but the *experience* of belief, in particular for a Jew like Shimen. So let's take a deep breath and have an unflinching look at what Shimen really believes.

* * *

Shimen's two children, Leibele and Chaya Sara, were taken from his hands and murdered. He witnessed countless friends who died *al kiddush Hashem* (sanctifying God's name) with the words of *Shema* or *Ani Maamin*, the most primal Jewish creeds, on their lips. He devotes his life to teaching young people about the suffering and the nobility of righteous Jews in the camps and ghettos.

I'll go out on a limb and suggest that Shimen holds no naive beliefs about God's benevolence and the worldly rewards bestowed upon those who follow in His ways. What, then, does Shimen believe?

Shimen believes, as deeply and as viscerally as one can believe anything, that the Jewish way – *Yiddishkeit* – is the life force that animates the Jewish people. He believes that this *Yiddishkeit* is what

---

1. Related points are made in Howard K. Wettstein, *The Significance of Religious Experience* (New York: Oxford University Press, 2012).

sets apart the Jews, whom he watched die with nothing left but an inner dignity rooted in their devotion to each other and to their shared way of life. He believes in his gut that *Yiddishkeit* – not vague professions of high-minded virtue, but *Yiddishkeit* in all its detail – is so fundamentally right that it must be God's will. He believes instinctively that devotion to the Jewish way is its own reward: he would not hesitate for a second to trade away the circumstances under which he lived, but he would not in a million years prefer to belong to any other people. And he believes that whatever is left of the Jews is sufficiently healthy at its core that it will regenerate and flourish.

Recall that Shimen's approach to halakha is principally mimetic; he has internalized the ways of his parents and his community. The halakhic codes are just for fine-tuning. The same is true of his beliefs, which are thoroughly internalized. For Shimen, codified principles of Jewish belief are just ways of expressing that internalized belief; he doesn't need them.

Still, if we were forced to codify Shimen's internalized belief as a set of assertions, what might the code look like?

Shimen's belief that the Jewish way expresses God's will could, for example, be codified as the claim that God revealed the Torah at some specific time and place. Shimen's belief that, whatever the circumstances, it is profoundly satisfying to be a God-fearing Jew might be codified as the claim that acting in accord with the Torah is rewarded and acting contrary to the Torah is punished. Shimen's belief in the fundamental viability of the Jewish way of life could plausibly be codified as the claim that collective loyalty to this way of life will ultimately lead to its ascendancy.

In short, at least one codified version of Shimen's ineffable beliefs would be more or less the set of claims that we're calling Jewish belief.

But this codified version doesn't capture what's going on in Shimen's mind; Shimen's belief is emotional, not intellectual. If you insist that he expound on his belief, he'll trot out the standard story, the one he learned in *ḥeder*. But the fact is that he hasn't got the slightest interest in exploring evidence for the veracity of any of the historical claims on which his most basic commitments ostensibly rely.

To understand why this is so, we need to understand the relationship between his internalized belief and his assent to the claims surrounding it. Think of it this way. Shimen loves his children, Leibele and Chaya Sara. He remembers them as sweet and innocent and wise beyond their years, almost angelic. But were they actually as angelic as he chooses to remember them? Were they never cranky or ornery, foolish or immature? Should Shimen undertake archival research and interviews of surviving neighbors to replace his fond memories of Leibele and Chaya Sara with more accurate ones?

I hope you see how utterly idiotic this is. Shimen doesn't love his children because they were angelic; he recalls them as angelic because he loves them. And recalling them this way only intensifies his love and his longing for them. Similarly, Jewish belief is only coherent and meaningful to those already committed to the Jewish way of life, who experience its vitality viscerally. For those who experience Jewish life as instinctively as Shimen, assent to codified Jewish belief might frame and intensify the experience, but is not the basis for that experience. And subjecting these claims to historical analysis makes as much sense to him as subjecting his memories of his children to historical analysis. Both his religious beliefs and his family memories are true for him not because of historical research but regardless of it.

Conversely, since these claims are merely outer expressions of inner experience, for those who don't share some form of this experience, the claims are empty shells. Attempting to prove the truth of the canonical Jewish historical narrative from outside Jewish practice is nothing but a fool's errand. In Judaism, belief can only be the residue of practice.

* * *

Someone as socialized as Shimen to the Jewish way of life can default to Jewish belief without giving it much thought. For Shimen, this default belief is simply part of his character; it's what we usually call *yirat shamayim* (fear of Heaven, in the sense of fear of God) – the Jewish way of referring to genuine religiosity. *Yirat shamayim* is almost orthogonal to the issue of one's opinions: you can formulate clever arguments in favor of Jewish belief and yet lack *yirat shamayim,* and you can formulate clever arguments against Jewish belief but nevertheless have *yirat shamayim.*

It should be obvious that the benefits of sustaining Jewish norms through belief accrue not from belief that is mere intellectual assent to claims, but instead from belief that is essentially *yirat shamayim.* To see how this plays out, let's very briefly consider the ways in which Jewish principles of belief, even as they arise out of Jewish practice, serve in turn to strengthen commitment to that very practice.

The belief that the Torah was revealed and so represents some transcendent truth implies that there is an objective moral order and a human capacity to live by it. It is this belief that instills in us the humility to respect tradition even in the face of our base inclinations and our grand moral theories. Moreover, it is this belief that renders coherent our moral intuitions regarding those flavors of morality besides fairness: restraint (*kedusha* and *tahara*) and loyalty (*kavod* and *yira*). As we saw in the first two parts of this book, respect for tradition and the broad scope of morality are the keys to Judaism's viability.

Similarly, the belief that good deeds are rewarded and bad deeds are punished, even if only in another world, incentivizes good deeds and disincentivizes bad ones. What is most important is the sense that one is being watched, rather than the salience of the punishment. The conviction that infractions are seen is so crucial to deterrence that experiments have shown that even the mere exposure to an image of a watching eye sometimes deters moral infractions or encourages pro-social behavior.[2] The belief in punishment in another world is a meaningful deterrent simply because it suggests that "there is an 'eye' that sees and an 'ear' that hears and all of one's actions are recorded."[3]

Finally, the belief in eventual redemption gives direction and purpose to a life lived in accord with the Torah. It orients the believer to a view in which the Jewish way is dynamic and not stagnant and in which a participant is advancing some larger historical process. A less appreciated point about formalized messianic belief is captured in the joke about the fellow who is offered to serve as sentinel entrusted with heralding the Messiah's arrival: it doesn't pay much, he's told, but it's steady work. The anticipatory nature of redemption in Jewish belief paradoxically softens eschatological fervor and prevents the calamities associated with "hastening the end" that afflict societies in which messianic longing is either too overt or too repressed.

Every one of these salutary consequences of belief results from *yirat shamayim* and not from intellectual assent to specific scientific or historical claims. Not for nothing is virtually all of classical Jewish literature prior to Saadia Gaon (tenth century) and Maimonides, who put forward creeds in the context of polemical responses to institutional challenges to tradition,[4] filled with

---

2. K. J. Haley and D. M. T. Fessler, "Nobody's Watching? Subtle Cues Affect Generosity in an Anonymous Economic Game," *Evolution and Human Behavior* 26 (2005): 245–56.

3. Mishna Avot 2:1.

4. For an anthology of attempts by medieval Spanish rabbis to codify traditional Jewish belief, including those of Saadia Gaon and Maimonides, see J. D. Bleich, *With Perfect Faith: Foundations of Jewish Belief* (New York: Ktav, 1983).

exhortations and narratives extolling the importance of *yirat shamayim* and almost free of discussion regarding the importance of assent to claims about the world – dogma. (Perhaps I overstate my case here: the Torah does make claims about how the world works, and, by implication, we are meant to take *some* of these claims literally. But the meta-discussion about the state of mind that the Torah wishes us to have is seldom about doctrine and always about *yirat shamayim*.)

Of course, we aren't all socialized quite as well as Shimen. We can't default to the belief that the society we belong to is a link in a directed process that connects our past with our future unless we have a very strong sense of which society we belong to: Gerer Hasidim, committed Jews, all Jews, educated Westerners, human beings, sentient beings? Similarly, no one has the luxury of simply defaulting to unstated beliefs that are grossly inconsistent with the foundations of the outside cultures with which we interact. In such cases, we might, for better or worse, be inclined to formulate our beliefs as explicit claims in much the way that Maimonides did.

I'll discuss the sociology of all this in the next part of the book. For now, the key point is that for Shimen, as well as for other committed Jews with more explicitly articulated traditional beliefs, Jewish belief is subordinate to action. Jewish belief motivates and frames commitment to Jewish norms and is meaningless in the absence of such commitment. If we define ideology as a commitment to specific beliefs about the world that precede and determine one's normative commitments, then Shimen's world is not an ideological one.

Chapter 11

The Need for Belief

Unlike Shimen, Heidi aspires to base her beliefs solely on evidence and to choose her commitments based on these justified beliefs. She specifically aspires for her most deeply held beliefs to transcend the particular culture in which she lives. But this aspiration must necessarily remain unfulfilled, because – as we will see – people can't live coherent lives without certain unfounded beliefs. And, in fact, for each of us, these necessary beliefs include beliefs inextricably tied to the particular culture in which we live.

BELIEFS THAT MAKE TRUTH POSSIBLE

Many arguments, some more persuasive and some less so, have been offered against the proposition that people have free will. Experiments by the neurologist Benjamin Libet[1] showed that a

---

1. Benjamin Libet, Curtis A. Gleason, Elwood W. Wright, Dennis K. Pearl, "Time of Conscious Intention to Act in Relation to Onset of Cerebral Activity (Readiness-Potential)," *Brain* 106, no. 3 (1983): 623–42.

subject's choice in a particular lab setting is preceded by detectable brain activity that foretells the subsequent choice. Some have argued that there are analytic complications: if all physical processes, including human action, are either deterministic or random, there is no room for willed action that is neither of those. Others point to numerous experiments showing that we are all subject to systemic biases of which we are unaware, so that an activity we regard as freely chosen is in fact stereotypical and predictable.

The merits of any of these arguments are not my concern here. The point is that regardless of how strong the arguments against free will are, you and I both believe that we have free will. If I were feeling ironic, I'd say that we don't really have a choice in the matter. But I'm not feeling ironic, so I'll say only that it is natural for us to believe that we have free will and it requires an act of will to think otherwise.

There are two separate, but connected, reasons why our belief in free will is inescapable. First, we experience our free will viscerally. Second, we can live coherent lives only by living as if we have free will.

This highlights the difference between beliefs and opinions. It might be my studied *opinion* that it's implausible that we have free will, but it's my *belief* that we do have free will. Our opinions are relevant to how we debate, but our beliefs are relevant to how we live our lives. Our beliefs are, in aggregate, like an operating system: they sit in the background and serve as a framework within which it is possible to organize our lives.

To push this point a bit further, let's think about scientific induction, the method that allows us to conclude that the sun will come up tomorrow and the moon will wane and wax this month. At the core of this method is the assumption that discernible patterns in nature can be generalized into laws that have held in the past and will continue to hold in the future.

How do we know? What basis do we have for this assumption? Well, you might argue that scientific induction has worked until now, so we have reason to expect that it will continue to work, but the circularity of that argument ought to be obvious. To appreciate this point, imagine asking an anti-inductivist, who holds that whatever was is exactly what will *not* be, what basis he has for believing that. If he's clever, he'll respond, "Well, it never worked until now." Furthermore, there is more than one way to generalize a discernible pattern. Maybe the law is that the sun comes up in the east every day only so long as the population of Tokyo doesn't exceed 15 million – which has not yet happened, but probably will soon – after which it comes up in the west on Jewish Holidays. Everything in our experience so far is consistent with this law.

And yet we all get up every day confidently expecting the floor to be there when we get out of bed and the sun to be inching its way up in the east. Clearly, we believe that whatever version of folk science we have in our heads is at least a crude guide to how the world works. In fact, I'm pretty certain that even the great Scottish philosopher David Hume, who first called attention to the difficulty of justifying scientific induction,[2] didn't put his hand on a lit stove just to see if fire still burns. As with free will, whatever our opinions regarding the justifiability of scientific induction, we *believe* that it works and live our lives accordingly. We could not do otherwise.

Finally, let's consider the assertion that some moral claims are objectively true in the same way that, for example, the claim that elephants are bigger than mice is objectively true. Do we have any basis for believing this? In fact, it's not difficult to rehearse the arguments against this assertion. Moral views depend on culture;

2. David Hume, *A Treatise of Human Nature* (Oxford, UK: Clarendon Press, 1739, 1888), book 1, 3:6.

they vary widely even among individuals in the same culture; they are usually vague even for a given individual. Moral statements can be interpreted as merely emotive (hurrah for charity, boo to child abuse) or imperative (give charity, don't beat children), rather than as claims about the world.

But even the philosophers most strongly opposed to moral realism don't hesitate to express moral opinions, usually regarding political matters, as if they take them quite seriously. (Also, they're usually good to their mothers.) When we say that charity is good and child abuse is bad, we mean exactly that and we mean it sincerely.[3] We believe these claims as strongly as we believe that elephants are bigger than mice. And, as with free will and scientific induction, we could not lead coherent lives without believing that some actions are morally preferable to others.

Free will, scientific induction, and morality are three issues that have generated voluminous literature but scant solid progress. That's because, however challenging the arguments for their inauthenticity may be, we necessarily believe that they are real. It is a myth that we seek truth for its own sake; we seek truth in order to live coherent lives. Whatever the truth about the reality of free will, scientific law, and morality, we cannot imagine living coherent lives without believing in that reality.

To make this pragmatic argument[4] a bit more fancifully, I can't prove that I'm not a character in *The Truman Show* or *The Matrix*; I can either simply believe that neither of these is the case

---

3. Michael Huemer, *Ethical Intuitionism* (London UK: Palgrave MacMillan, 2005).

4. The term "pragmatic" here is meant to evoke similar arguments proposed by William James, most notably in W. James, *The Will to Believe and Other Popular Essays in Philosophy* (Cambridge, MA: Harvard University Press, 1897, 1979), and W. James, *Pragmatism: A New Name for Some Old Ways of Thinking* (Cambridge, MA: Harvard University Press 1907, 1975). My argument differs from his in that he argues only that some ideas are true "just in so far as they help us to get into satisfactory relation with other parts of our experience," while I argue that some ideas are prerequisites for the pursuit of truth.

or I can waste my life paralyzed by suspicion and uncertainty. We will soon see that we hold quite a few of these necessary beliefs.

Lest I be misunderstood, I want to clarify the relationship between necessary beliefs and truth. I'm not suggesting that necessary beliefs are false but we ought to hold them anyway because they make us feel good. I'm arguing that we can only begin to seek truth from within some framework that allows us to organize experience. In this sense, that basic framework is unfalsifiable.

BELIEFS THAT MAKE MEANING POSSIBLE

The beliefs we just considered – the reality of free will, scientific induction, and morality – do not exhaust the list of necessary beliefs. Let's consider one more such necessary belief, one that will take us one step closer toward understanding the meaning of canonical Jewish beliefs.

Suppose that, as a result of some natural disaster, all human beings have become sterile. Once those alive today live out their lives, the human race will end. This scenario, contemplated by the writer P. D. James in her novel *The Children of Men*,[5] is the basis of a thought experiment considered by the philosopher Samuel Scheffler.[6]

Scheffler's "afterlife conjecture" is that the knowledge that the human race has no long-term future would already suck all the life out of us. Clearly, we'd no longer see any point in engaging in activities, like long-term research projects, infrastructure development, reform of public institutions, or international diplomacy, that are meant to pay off only in the distant future. But, Scheffler asserts, we would actually lose our taste even for activities that ostensibly give us pleasure in the here and now, like the consumption of music, art, food, and sex. That is because our pleasure from

---

5. P. D. James, *The Children of Men* (London, UK: Faber and Faber, 1992).

6. S. Scheffler, *Death and Afterlife* (Oxford, UK: Oxford University Press, 2013).

these activities depends on their embeddedness in our lives as wholes, and more broadly on our lives' embeddedness in ongoing human history. In short, the value we ascribe to everything we do assumes that we are each links in some ongoing chain of human life.

I'm persuaded that Scheffler is right, but his conjecture does not go far enough. To see why, let's entertain some variations on the thought experiment. Suppose that the event that precipitated this calamity spared the fertility of an aboriginal tribe in the forests of New Guinea. In fact, suppose that most of the human population would be spared, except for anyone who even remotely shared your culture. It's safe to surmise that even in the case of such more limited calamities, the problem that Scheffler presents would not be significantly mitigated; you'd still find that your life had lost its purpose and that even pistachio ice cream didn't quite taste the same. If, for example, you were the last Jew on earth, you'd probably find shaking a lulav and etrog an empty experience, even on Sukkot (the Holiday during which these plants are traditionally put to ritual use).

Or is that wrong? After all, many people, like Shimen, face life knowing that they will not leave behind any living descendants, and yet forge on and live meaningful and directed lives. What are we to make of all this?

Apparently, for our lives to have meaning, the continuity of human life as a whole is not sufficient and the proliferation of our own flesh-and-blood descendants is not necessary. What, then, is both necessary and sufficient? I propose this: Each of us must believe in the viability of the culture of which we are a part. Precisely because of our awareness of our own mortality, we would be paralyzed by dread if we did not believe that we are engaged in some project that connects that which has preceded us with that which will succeed us and that gives context and direction to everything we do. In other words, we need to transcend our narrow self-interest by situating ourselves in a process that includes other people and extends beyond the here and now. This kind of self-transcendence is the linchpin that connects virtue with human flourishing.[7] What is debilitating for us, then, is the loss of belief in the viability of that project, our culture, for the long-term.

We saw above that we each necessarily harbor an implicit belief in the reality of free will, scientific law, and morality because we couldn't organize our lives any other way. We can now add to the list of necessary beliefs the belief that the culture within which we organize our lives is viable for the long-term future. Just as we can't begin to organize our lives without first believing that the world is at least partially predictable, that we are capable of choosing a direction in life, and that some directions are better than others, we must also believe that there are long-term consequences to the choices we make.

This necessary belief in the viability of our own culture is analogous in several ways to the necessary beliefs we considered earlier. Just as our beliefs in the reality of free will, scientific law, and morality are experiential and are conceptually prior to our opinions, so too, our belief in the viability of our own culture is experiential: we experience our culture as a living and directed one.

In Shimen's case, the substance of his religious belief is, as we have seen, precisely the experience of Judaism as a living and directed culture. Given his commitment to Judaism, Shimen's belief is simply the minimum necessary to give his life direction and meaning; it requires no further defense.

But even for Shimen, the substance of this belief has to conform to his experience of the world. This is even truer for those who, unlike Shimen, prefer to think more concretely of the claim that Judaism is a uniquely viable process. As I have argued throughout this book, Jewish tradition has indeed proved itself to

---

7. J. Frey and C. Vogler, *Self-Transcendence and Virtue: Perspective from Philosophy, Psychology, and Theology* (Oxfordshire, UK: Routledge, 2018).

be viable over millennia; it is well adapted to human moral intuitions, carefully balancing the universal and particularist flavors of morality; it strikes a balance between a living oral tradition and a written tradition of analysis and codification. If you had to bet on the viability of one culture – and, by the way, you do – you could do worse than putting your money on the Jews. I very much doubt you could do better.

In the words of Mark Twain:

> The Egyptian, the Babylonian, and the Persian rose, filled the planet with sound and splendor, then faded to dream-stuff and passed away; the Greek and the Roman followed, and made a vast noise, and they are gone; other peoples have sprung up and held their torch high for a time, but it burned out, and they sit in twilight now, or have vanished. The Jew saw them all, beat them all, and is now what he always was, exhibiting no decadence, no infirmities of age, no weakening of his parts, no slowing of his energies, no dulling of his alert and aggressive mind. All things are mortal but the Jew; all other forces pass, but he remains.[8]

To summarize, Shimen's belief is subsequent to his moral commitments, is a version of the minimum necessary belief given those commitments, and isn't implausible. Do these observations apply as well to the beliefs of Heidi and Amber? Let's see.

---

8. Mark Twain, "Concerning the Jews," *Harper's Magazine* 99 (1899): 527–35.

Chapter 12

The Perils of Ideology

In many ways, Heidi's approach to belief is not all that different from Shimen's. She too is committed to a particular culture and believes in the continued flourishing of her own society. But, unlike Shimen, Heidi is persuaded that it is possible and desirable to base fundamental beliefs about the world on reason alone. The result of this unreasonable optimism, as we shall see, is not the proliferation of rationality, but rather a society of Ambers in the grip of anti-rational ideology.

Let's first consider what it means for Heidi to believe in the flourishing of her own culture and society. Heidi has rejected the fairly traditional society in which she was raised in favor of the more cosmopolitan society with which she now identifies. Her chosen path has direction and meaning only in light of particular beliefs about human nature that make the continuing spread of cosmopolitanism both desirable and likely. Thus, for example, Heidi believes that apparent differences in average ability or achievement among different populations are either illusory or the result of discrimination, exploitation, and oppression; "culture" is never an explanatory factor. Similarly, she believes that most apparent differences between genders are socially constructed and not rooted in human nature, and that overcoming these socially constructed differences is both feasible and harmless. Heidi believes that traditional institutions that encourage cultural distinctiveness and self-segregation are nothing but barriers to universal sisterhood and that abandoning them in favor of new institutions expertly designed for the perfection of humankind will lead to a more peaceful and prosperous world.

In short, Heidi's beliefs are in direct contradiction with the arguments I made in the first two parts of this book on behalf of the necessity for traditional social norms manifesting all three moral foundations. But never mind if these beliefs are borne out by evidence. Like Shimen's beliefs, Heidi's beliefs are primarily intended to give meaning to her moral commitments rather than to create these commitments, and – again like Shimen – Heidi isn't actually very invested in establishing the truth of her beliefs in any conventional sense.

In fact, although Heidi raised her daughter Amber on these beliefs, they are rather marginal in her own operative view of the world. Heidi lives a rather segregated, elitist, and conventional life that for the most part reflects the values on which she was raised. She might find it unseemly to blame culture for the failures of certain populations, but these days she doesn't seek or have much to do with those populations or their cultures. She might regard gender differences as socially constructed and overcome-able, but she has mostly internalized those differences and lives accordingly. She might find traditional norms divisive, but she often feels uneasy violating them. In short, Heidi can afford to parade her anti-traditional convictions at little cost because she takes so much of tradition for granted.

Amber is a different story. Amber has been raised on Heidi's anti-traditional commitments without the benefit of the traditional background that Heidi takes for granted. Amber senses that, unlike Heidi, she has no heritage from which to define a trajectory into the future, not even one to rebel against. She doesn't have conventional choices to default to, so her life is an unending series of burdensome decisions. She is jealous of her third-world friends, who were raised with defined identities and traditions that they can either flaunt or overcome. Amber is angry even about the life of banal privilege that denies her the cachet of victimhood.

Heidi's unfounded, if harmless, ideas about human nature have led to Amber's considerably less benign beliefs. Lacking any tradition to draw on, Amber and her colleagues have essentially invented a new religion founded not on a shared moral heritage but rather on imaginary shared persecution and shared doctrines of recent vintage. These doctrines don't merely give meaning to a prior moral heritage – as do Shimen's beliefs and, to some extent, Heidi's – they are actually the basis of a new moral absolutism. Amber is an ideologue.

Amber takes seriously Heidi's precept that all differences in outcomes between different groups must be the result of oppression. She devotes significant effort to identifying successful communities to penalize and alleged victims to patronize and proselytize. Amber takes seriously Heidi's belief in the absence of essential differences between genders, so she rejects gender dichotomy altogether. She demands that the state regulate private speech and behavior to obliterate the very memory of binary gender, *inter alia* by magnifying the extent and significance of transgenderism and other such relatively rare phenomena. Amber takes seriously Heidi's belief that traditional norms are divisive. In the name of universal sisterhood, she seeks to destabilize precisely those traditional virtues that are common to all societies and that make cross-cultural harmony possible. Like many true believers, Amber wishes to use the power of the state and the wrath of the mob to silence heretics and banish idolaters.

Note the important difference between Shimen's belief in the viability of a normative system to which he has a prior commitment and the ideological beliefs that *shape* Amber's normative commitments. If Shimen's beliefs are wrong, well... let me tell a joke. An aspiring young *apikoros* (heretic) travels from the shtetl to see how the famed veteran *apikoros* of Warsaw spends his Shabbat. Much to his surprise, he endures a long Shabbat during which the old *apikoros* observes every ritual and every restriction down to the last detail. He expresses his astonishment, and when the old *apikoros* asks what he expected, he responds that he expected the old fellow to wantonly violate the Shabbat rules. "Why should I do that?" asks the old *apikoros*. "What do you mean? *Lehakhis!*" – out of spite. With a bewildered look, the old *apikoros* simply shrugs and says, "To spite Whom?"

In the absence of a compelling reason to act otherwise, maintaining one's traditions is a perfectly natural and harmless default. Contrast this with Amber's ideology. If she turns out to be wrong and traditional institutions matter in ways that Amber did not anticipate, societies that bet their futures on Amber's ideological doctrines are liable to come apart at the seams.

Traditional belief, like Shimen's, gives the moral life direction, depth, and meaning. Those who abandon such belief often err in taking for granted the moral virtues that it bolsters. The loss of that belief and those virtues does not lead, as Heidi would have us suppose, to a life of rationality and clear-eyed reason, but rather to beliefs less tempered by the hard-earned wisdom of the ages and to norms less amenable to sustaining a viable, thriving, moral community and tradition. Heidi can live off the dividends of the moral capital of the world she left; not so Amber.

* * *

The key takeaway of Part 3 is that certain beliefs are inescapable prerequisites for the very search for truth and meaning. Among these are that the world is intelligible, that there are right and wrong actions, that we can choose what to do, and that our society is sufficiently viable that our individual and collective choices have long-term consequences. Societies, like Shimen's, that can sustain this last belief in a way that stirs the heart and satisfies the intellect can live with direction and meaning; those that can't are liable to turn to brittle and short-lived ideologies as substitutes.

The arguments presented here are somewhat preliminary, but they suggest that exploration of the scope and precise nature of necessary beliefs could serve as an organizing principle for a fruitful research program.

Shimen held very sober beliefs. But, it's time to deal with a glaring fact that I've deliberately set aside until now: Shimen is long gone and he has left behind no children. This isn't merely a sad biographical detail; it signifies the broader fact that Shimen's whole world is gone. What, then, comes next? Can Shimen's kind of Judaism be revived? This is the topic of Part 4.

PART 4

Where Are We Headed?

In the fourth and final part of the book, we'll consider the future of Shimen's kind of Judaism. The questions we'll address include: Why does Shimen's organic Judaism seem to be disappearing? Can it be revived under contemporary conditions, and what might it look like? What are its prospects in the United States? What are its prospects in Israel?

Chapter 13

Traditionalism as Equilibrium

One winter afternoon just a few years after my conversation with Heidi at Princeton, I stood in front of the central Gerer study hall in Jerusalem waiting for the hearse transporting Shimen's casket from Ben Gurion Airport to the Mount of Olives. The hearse paused for a few moments in front of the study hall so that the Gerer Rebbe could briefly mumble a few words in Shimen's honor to the usual gaggle of hangers-on. The throngs who would have come to honor Shimen on his final journey were all long murdered or had never been born.

Shimen left behind no surviving children, but many of his friends in the Gerer *shtiebel* did. Some of their children, typically the first ones born after The War, somehow failed to appreciate having the weight of a million dead children on their shoulders and moved as far away as they could. Others, often the youngest in the family, understood an unspoken message and chose to return to traditional hasidic dress – *bekeshe* and *spodek*. Most grew up to be *heimish* and *balabatish* (two Yiddish terms roughly suggesting bourgeois familial virtues, but lacking American equivalents, linguistically or conceptually) like their parents, but still not quite the same.

Let's face it. What was special about Shimen and his cronies was, to some extent, the product of very specific and tragic circumstances. They had lived in a closed world and then seen it destroyed. On the one hand, their *Yiddishkeit* was deeply ingrained and fully internalized; on the other hand, having been robbed of their families and communities, they were as independent and self-determining as human beings could be. They had no need to impress anybody or to signal loyalty, and they held no illusions. In short, they were authentic in ways that most others can't afford to be.

So, let's confront the question that I've been eliding since the very beginning of this book. Is there any empirical reason to believe that Shimen's traditionalism is, under current circumstances, any more viable than Heidi and Amber's progressivism? This will be the subject of the fourth part of the book.

We'll be leaving Shimen behind and taking a sober look at the development over the past few decades of those American and Israeli Jewish communities that still claim the mantle of tradition. The key grounds for pessimism regarding American and other diaspora communities, as we'll see in the following chapter, are that the forces at work in these communities seem to be entirely centrifugal. That sweet spot in the center, in which Shimen could be free of illusions but still unapologetically deeply traditional, is becoming virtually uninhabitable. The confrontation with the world outside the community's walls – Heidi's world and, subsequently, Amber's world – has forced many of Shimen's would-be descendants to choose between stultifying segregation and abject accommodation. The center cannot hold.

Similar, though not quite identical, problems plague Jewish communities in Israel; we'll discuss these in Chapter 15.

This raises an obvious problem for the thesis I've been developing throughout this book. If Shimen's way of life is viable and Heidi's is not, as I have been arguing, why does it look as if Heidi's cosmopolitan world is thriving, while Shimen's is disappearing? To answer this question, we first need to be a bit more precise about what exactly is entailed by the term "viable," which I've been tossing around rather loosely until now.

We can start with a better-defined concept that we've met several times above: equilibrium. We've considered equilibria in the Prisoner's Dilemma and in coordination problems. In each case, participating players' strategies are said to (jointly) constitute an equilibrium if neither player would change his strategy given that the other player would not change his strategy. More generally, we say that some system is in equilibrium if there is no *inherent* reason that the state of the system must change over time.

For example, the human body is in equilibrium at a temperature of 37°C. This temperature can in principle be maintained indefinitely. If, for external reasons, this temperature is pushed up or down, the body's internal thermostat will kick in to pull it back to its equilibrium state: in the case of overheating, sweating cools us down, and in the case of overcooling, shivering warms us up. For exactly this reason, the body cannot maintain any temperature other than 37°C for long; thus, we say that other body temperatures are not equilibria.

So, to restate the main argument of this book, Shimen's traditionalism constitutes an equilibrium, but Heidi's cosmopolitanism does not.

To be sure, I'm not saying that traditionalism is perfectly static. Rather, just as body temperature rises and falls in response to stimuli but is pulled back to its equilibrium temperature by internal regulatory mechanisms, traditionalism too can be thrown off its game by external stimuli but finds its way back to its equilibrium state. Nor am I suggesting that traditionalism doesn't suffer losses.

Indeed, more Jews, like Heidi, have defected from traditional Judaism than have stayed.

My claim is simply that Heidi's cosmopolitanism, but not Shimen's traditional Judaism, suffers from an internal dynamic that guarantees that it will undermine its own central features. I've devoted the bulk of this book to explaining why I believe this is the case, but let's put the various strands of the argument together now.

The roots of Heidi's worldview are found in two principles of the Enlightenment: religious tolerance and the centrality of reason and science. Both of these values brought a great deal of benefit to the world generally and to traditional Jews, like the ancestors of Shimen and Heidi, in particular. Tolerance brought a greater measure of security and freedom to religious and ethnic minorities and others. Science and technology, in combination with capitalism and free markets, advanced health and longevity, prosperity and convenience, and much more. Whatever differences there are today between Shimen and Heidi, they are not about the religious tolerance and scientific advances that yielded these benefits.

Religious tolerance does not entail the belief that all religions are equally valid (or invalid). Nor does an appreciation of scientific method entail the denial of any conclusions reached by means other than observation and reason, such as tradition or intuition. Here, for example, are the words of one of the earliest and most important Enlightenment philosophers, John Locke: "But natural religion, in its full extent, was nowhere, that I know, taken care of by the force of natural reason. It should seem, by the little that has hitherto been done in it, that 'tis too hard a task for unassisted reason, to establish morality, in all its parts, upon its true foundations, with a clear and convincing light."[1]

---

1. John Locke, *The Reasonableness of Christianity*, ed. J. Higgins-Biddle (Oxford, UK: Clarendon, 1695, 2000), 148.

Indeed, for all of Enlightenment thinkers' opposition to the Church's coercive power and some of its doctrines, almost everyone at that time still engaged the world from within some sort of religious community. The moral foundations of religion, as well as religious narratives about history, human nature, and meaning, still served as the background for their worldviews.

But as tolerance and reason squeezed out other values, traditional social attachments were gradually subverted. Thus, tolerance and reason employed from *within* a particular religious or national perspective began to give way to what might be called "the view from nowhere." Migrations, urbanization, and the breakdown of religious institutions led to a previously unknown phenomenon of whole societies, concentrated in ethnically heterogeneous metropolitan areas, constituted largely of individuals lacking connection with any religious community or narrative. As some would put it, for them the world had become "disenchanted"[2] or "desacralized."[3]

This is the point at which Shimen and Heidi part ways. Heidi's positions, as described above, follow not *directly* from an emphasis on tolerance and reason, but rather from the corrosion of moral communities subsequent to the rise of tolerance and reason. Without communities to inculcate specific virtues and the rules for cultivating them, all of morality is reduced to theories of fairness; without communities to maintain traditions and organically aggregate individual moral intuitions, social choice must be left to bureaucrats; without communal narratives and aspirations, hope for shared meaning and purpose is depleted.

---

2. The term originates in a 1917 lecture of Max Weber, subsequently translated into English and published as Max Weber, "Science as a Vocation," in *From Max Weber: Essays in Sociology*, trans. and ed. H. H. Gerth and C. Wright Mills (New York: Oxford University Press, 1946). See also Steven D. Smith, *The Disenchantment of Secular Discourse* (Cambridge, MA: Harvard University Press, 2010).

3. Mircea Eliade, *The Sacred and the Profane* (New York: Harcourt, 1959).

This disenchanted world comprised of individuals without religious communities is the one that is not in equilibrium. Bereft of tradition, individuals can't simply reason their way to rules that encourage virtue, and they can't spontaneously develop a strong sense of common purpose. Individual autonomy is reduced to mere self-indulgence and self-centeredness, social capital diminishes, and social bonds fray. The fortitude to raise children dissipates.[4] In the best case, Heidi can coast on the benefits of the social solidarity and virtues on which she was raised and free-ride on the efforts of traditionalists like Shimen to keep them alive.[5]

Moreover, even the very freedom that Heidi ostensibly wishes to strengthen is in fact diminished, because when virtues are undervalued, the need for powerful institutions to rein people in is increased. As Edmund Burke put it: "Society cannot exist unless a controlling power upon will and appetite be placed somewhere, and the less of it there is within, the more there must be without."[6] In the absence of moral communities to do the job, those with political power step in. And those with political power have an interest in further weakening civil-society institutions that could challenge them; they are thus well served both by state welfare, which weakens familial obligations, and by moral relativism, which weakens communal commitments. Under such conditions,

---

4. According to World Values Survey data, there is only a single country (Israel) in the OECD in which women who self-describe as secular are reproducing at or above replacement level. See Eric Kaufmann, *Shall the Religious Inherit the Earth?* (London UK: Profile Books, 2010).

5. Of course, Heidi would counter that people like Shimen often free-ride on the benefits of technology and tolerance. Fair enough, but grievance competitions are not my concern here. The key point for my purposes is that Shimen's society has already proved that, if need be, it can either survive without these benefits or contribute to them without compromising its character. Heidi's society has not yet demonstrated that it can survive for long without the residue of traditionalism.

6. Edmund Burke, *Further Reflections on the Revolution in France* (Indianapolis, IN: Liberty Fund, 1790, 1992), 69.

many willingly yield their freedom. In Tocqueville's words: "When the religion of a people is destroyed, doubt gets hold of the highest portions of the intellect, and half paralyzes all the rest of its powers.... Such a condition cannot but enervate the soul, relax the springs of the will, and prepare a people for servitude."[7] As we have seen above, these insights of Burke and Tocqueville have proved prescient.

In short, Heidi's secular cosmopolitanism undermines itself; it does not constitute an equilibrium.

If Heidi's secular cosmopolitanism is self-undermining, what comes after it? To understand the possibilities, consider another critique of secular cosmopolitanism. We have argued here that the quest for justice and truth is a process that unfolds within a given tradition. A community collectively fine-tunes its social norms in response to changing circumstances, and its members find meaning within a narrative that connects the community's past to its future. In this sense, justice and truth are, as the philosopher Alasdair MacIntyre puts it, at least partially "tradition-constituted."[8] Thus, another possible critique of secular cosmopolitanism is that its own underlying assumptions about truth and justice are parochial, and attempts to impose them universally are simply imperialistic.

This is a critique that is shared by religious traditionalists like MacIntyre and a diverse host of recent critics often lumped together as "postmodernists."[9] But traditionalists and postmodernists draw opposite conclusions from this critique. For MacIntyre, the upshot of the partial dependency of justice and truth on

---

7. Alexis de Tocqueville, *Democracy in America*, vol. 2, 1:5 (1840).
8. Alasdair MacIntyre, *Whose Justice? Which Rationality?* (South Bend, IN: Notre Dame University Press, 1988). MacIntyre makes considerable effort to distinguish this tradition dependency from mere relativism.
9. For example, Michel Foucault, "Truth and Power," in *Essential Works of Foucault*, ed. James D. Faubion, vol. 3: *Power* (New York: The New Press, 1979).

tradition is that one must choose a tradition – and not just any tradition, but rather one that is in equilibrium in the sense that I have described here. There's no "just plain soup," and not every kind of soup is good.

By contrast, the upshot of the postmodern critique of Heidi's secular cosmopolitanism, as internalized by Amber and her friends, is the dismantling of what little shared civilization remains in Heidi's world. Having cottoned on to the pretensions of secular cosmopolitanism but lacking any alternative tradition, postmodernists like Amber regard traditional social norms, and often even the conventions of scientific inquiry, as nothing but vehicles for the powerful to subjugate the weak. Such postmodernists undermine solidarity within communities by fomenting dissension along lines of race and gender, and they construe the pursuit of objective truth as nothing but cultural construction. Their indiscriminate subversiveness runs exactly counter to the enlightenment project of tolerance and rationality that served as the foundation of Heidi's worldview.

Amber's postmodernism will not get Heidi back to equilibrium.

The thrust of my argument in the first three parts of this book is that unlike Heidi's cosmopolitanism, Shimen's traditionalism constitutes an equilibrium. The balance of moral foundations, the unregulated combination of aggregated moral intuitions with expert reasoning, and the narrative that captures shared meaning and purpose are, in tandem, self-sustaining.

But the mechanism through which this is achieved is by no means simple. For Judaism to endure, there must be a cadre of people like Shimen who are guided by a clear-eyed and internalized trust in its viability. Such trust is possible only if Judaism's content is relatively stable over time, while very gradually adapting to changing circumstances by being responsive to the intuitions of its practitioners. This combination of stability and adaptability depends in turn on Shimen and others balancing the humility to submit to received tradition with confidence in their own intuitions to resolve matters at the fuzzy edges of halakha. This balance of humility and confidence is possible only if Shimen's received Judaism cultivates the full range of moral foundations, including those, like loyalty and restraint, that depend on fidelity to a specific culture, as well as those, like fairness, that are more universal. Sustaining this range of moral foundations depends on people like Shimen acquiring and bequeathing requisite culture-specific knowledge, as well as on well-honed intuitions rooted in that acquired knowledge. But – now closing the circle – Shimen and others will make the necessary effort to acquire this knowledge, fine-tune these intuitions, and pass this knowledge to future generations only if Judaism merits their trust in its own viability.

This is a delicate mechanism and it is easy to see that the whole system can easily be thrown out of equilibrium. Shimen studied enough to have deep and broad knowledge of Torah and was sufficiently uncompromised socially and intellectually to retain intuitions and attitudes deeply rooted in that knowledge. His knowledge of Judaism was sufficient to develop humility toward that body of received wisdom, and his intuitions were sharp enough to give him confidence in his own ability to add to it. To some extent this was possible because he lived in a tight-knit community that was in many senses an autonomous island in a hostile and unwelcoming environment. Are these the only circumstances under which such qualities of character can be developed? Do you need to be a cranky old Polish Jew to get Judaism right?

In the following two chapters, we'll consider all the reasons to be skeptical. We'll see that in both America and Israel the essential elements of Shimen's traditionalism seem be on the decline. But the crucial question, which we'll address in the book's final chapter, is not the current state of traditional Judaism, but rather whether its homeostatic mechanisms will bring it back to its equilibrium state.

Chapter 14

Centrifugal Forces

If we're to understand the direction in which observant Jewish communities in America are headed, we'll first need to overcome one common misconception. Communities of observant Jews in the United States, Israel, and other places are commonly characterized as being either Modern Orthodox (in Israel, this group is often called national-religious) or *ḥaredi* (non-modern Orthodox). Those who identify as *ḥaredi* tend to be stricter about certain aspects of halakha and to hold more uncompromising views on particular religious matters. Many people today imagine that this binary division is some sort of immutable law of nature that always has been and always will be. Given that dichotomy, they put Shimen in the *ḥaredi* box. But in fact Shimen was completely unaware of any such dichotomy, and the attempt to shoehorn him into such a box is anachronistic.

Yes, Shimen spoke Yiddish and prayed in a hasidic *shtiebel*. He was not acculturated into American society and was suspicious of all sorts of characters outside his community. To the poorly informed contemporary observer, he seems *ḥaredi*. But, on the substance, he pre-dated the institutional split within the world of observant Judaism between what are now called Modern Orthodox and *haredi* societies.

Consider some of the issues that, for better or worse, are now commonly regarded as litmus tests for membership in one or the other of these societies. Is an advanced secular education essential for living an integrated Jewish life, or is it a gateway to acculturation and assimilation? Is Zionism a step in the redemptive process, or a secular revolt against religion? Are stringencies in halakha showy overreaches, or commendable precautions? Are leading rabbis simply experts in halakha, or oracular fonts of wisdom in all areas? We can go on and on, but this will do.

Shimen was not a party to any of this. He was a practical man. In Shimen's view, if you think an education will get you ahead in life, go ahead and get one – as long as you also learn Torah. A sovereign Jewish state is probably good for the Jews, whether or not it's a step in the redemptive process. Some halakhic stringencies are better, some are worse; suit yourself. In the worst of times, rabbis often exhibited inspiring righteousness and sometimes even profound heroism, but political acumen is not necessarily part of their repertoire.

In other words, Shimen's Judaism is commonsensical and organic. And that's the key.

Now, it's not as if Shimen didn't have his biases. But his division of the Jewish world cut through an altogether different axis from the customary modern/*haredi* axis. For Shimen, there were Polish Jews, the thoughtful and cantankerous types who defined the norm for him, and an assortment of other types, each of whom suffered from some stereotypical flaw. These included Lithuanian-Jewish Litvaks (learned, but cold and elitist), Hungarians (warmer, but overly concerned with appearances), German-Jewish *Yekkes* (upright and uptight), and, at the bottom of the totem pole, *Amerikaners* (earnest and eager, but naive and Jewishly ignorant). Shimen carried his resentments around with him, but if you were learned and a *mensch*, he didn't judge you too harshly on the details.

It was not only Shimen who didn't choose sides on the modern/*haredi* axis. A generation of yeshiva-educated baby boomers growing up after The War moved comfortably along the spectrum running from Orthodox and segregated to modern and assimilating. On the one hand, they inherited deep feelings of alienation and resentment toward oblivious American Jews and their smug establishment. On the other hand, as is common with children of immigrants, they rushed headlong into professional achievement and American culture, often including the 1960s counter-culture. The resulting tension played out in many interesting ways, including various singular combinations that are fast becoming extinct.

These days there are no top-tier yeshiva heads playing chess at the opera. There are no wives of hasidic rebbes studying in Hunter College and no future hasidic rebbes getting educated in modern day schools. There are no leading students of old-school yeshiva heads simultaneously teaching philosophy in university or moonlighting as troubadours in Greenwich Village. But in New York in the 1960s, all these characters existed. And none of them thought of themselves as renegades; their paths seem unusual now, in fact downright impossible, but were perfectly natural not that long ago.

To be sure, such free spirits are typical of the chaos that attends dislocation and the ferment that precedes the development of institutions. Segregation into distinct subcommunities is an indication of communal maturity and has been common throughout Jewish history. But there is often a price to pay for this maturation. To understand the currency in which this price is paid, consider how the process of segregation plays out.

The rapid growth of Orthodox institutions in America after The War, especially beginning in the late sixties and seventies, has had some unintended consequences. Large educational institutions are not artisanal studios; they are instruments of mass production. Since such institutions compete for students, they inevitably cluster around certain standard forms. In the case of yeshiva day schools, these clusters were, at the lowest level of granularity, Modern Orthodox and *haredi*. Even if many graduates of these institutions ultimately chose their own divergent paths, these yeshivas and schools came to define a standard against which everyone in the relevant communities has had to self-define. Eventually these institutions were around long enough to produce their own teachers, creating a feedback loop that narrowed and hardened institutional identity. Graduates of the various standard educational types have sorted themselves out to different neighborhoods, like the Modern Orthodox town of Teaneck, New Jersey, and the *haredi* Boro Park neighborhood in Brooklyn, where there is intense pressure to conform to the appropriate stereotype and where opportunities for interaction across communities have become limited. The division of a messy continuum into distinct subcommunities has thus led to increasing polarization.

The axis along which such polarization takes place is easy to identify. Observant Jews in an open society dominated by Heidi's values need to make choices. To what extent ought they take advantage of the opportunities that Heidi's world offers, and to what extent ought they segregate themselves to avoid its temptations?

Shimen could afford to be rather blasé and pragmatic about such matters. While he was very appreciative of the openness of American society and the freedom it gave him to live as he chose, American culture was for the most part nothing more than background music for him. It didn't penetrate too deeply into his world, so he didn't need to react to it beyond the occasional *krechtz* (groan). Shimen was sufficiently rooted in his own culture not to feel threatened by Heidi's culture. But Shimen's indifference to Heidi's world is not characteristic of a younger generation of observant Jews growing up in the United States.

YITZY AND BEN

Let's meet two cousins: Yitzy (whom we met briefly in Chapter 6) and Ben, both of whom were, like Heidi, born in the early 1960s, the last of the baby boomers. Unlike Heidi, Yitzy and Ben grew up in Brooklyn, and their parents were Polish survivors who shared sensibilities similar to those of Shimen. Their mothers were sisters, the only survivors in their extended family, and they lived a few blocks away from each other.

Yitzy and Ben grew up in a Jewish ghetto inside one of the most cosmopolitan cities in the world. Though encouraged to avoid pop culture, they were surrounded by it wherever they went. The boys sometimes studied Torah together, talked baseball ad nauseam ("Stottlemyre's not in Seaver's league, what's the *hava amina*!?" Yitzy would say, using the talmudic term for a discarded initial interpretation), and shared Hardy Boys books. Both attended boys-only yeshiva elementary schools and high schools that taught secular studies in the afternoon.

But, like two raindrops falling on a mountain ridge that randomly run down opposite sides of the mountain, Ben and Yitzy grew apart. For reasons of mere convenience, Ben attended schools that defined themselves as Zionist and invested time and effort in general education, while Yitzy attended schools that rarely mentioned Israel and complied in a somewhat resigned manner with state requirements to provide a general education. After their bar mitzvas, Yitzy began to dress *yeshivish*, always wearing a white button-down shirt and dark pants, while Ben preferred a more modern look. After high school, Yitzy continued on to advanced Talmud study, and Ben went off to Columbia University.

These days Ben and Yitzy have little in common beyond baseball and they rarely meet or speak. Yitzy married the daughter of the head of the yeshiva he attended and spent a good number of years after marriage studying Torah full-time, before taking a job as an insurance agent. He and his wife have raised their six children with very limited secular education. They live in an Orthodox enclave in Brooklyn and their lives revolve around local Jewish institutions with which they are affiliated; they take little interest in general affairs that don't directly affect their community.

Ben married late, after finishing law school and establishing himself as a Wall Street lawyer. He and his wife, a fashion designer, have raised their three children to appreciate contemporary culture and to enthusiastically pursue professional advancement. They live in a tony New Jersey suburb and are members in a local Modern Orthodox synagogue, which Ben often attends on Shabbat mornings. Both Ben and his wife are deeply committed to their careers and have strong opinions on public policy issues.

What is it about Orthodox life in America that makes the sharp bifurcation between Yitzy and Ben almost inevitable? Why is Shimen's rooted and balanced fidelity to tradition not a stable state in an environment dominated by Heidis? The answer, I believe, is this: unlike Shimen, who didn't feel a need to impress his friends and didn't feel culturally threatened by larger American society, both Yitzy and Ben are always aware of and playing to two audiences – the observant Jewish world inside the ghetto and the cosmopolitan world outside the ghetto. There are two different strategies available for ameliorating this inside-outside tension: segregation and accommodation. Yitzy chose segregation and Ben chose accommodation.

Let's consider Yitzy's segregation and Ben's accommodation, respectively, and see why neither is quite like Shimen's organic Judaism.

Precisely because Heidi's world is accessible and tempting to him, Yitzy chooses not to provide his children with the sort of education that yields social capital more easily redeemed outside than inside their community. Expertise in Torah is best rewarded within his society, while academic achievements will always be valued and rewarded outside his society. Yitzy is afraid that if his kids get too good a secular education, they'll ultimately give their allegiance to the society that best appreciates the skills they have to offer. While Shimen valued Torah study more than he did academic achievement, he was not defensive about secular knowledge and didn't underestimate its worth.

Yitzy is meticulous about even the apparently trivial details of halakha. He is careful to be no less exacting with seemingly arbitrary traditions than he is with more intuitive traditions. He avoids prettifying halakha by smoothing its jagged edges. So far, so good; Shimen would be completely sympathetic to this attitude. The problem is that Yitzy isn't merely careful not to slight arbitrary-seeming traditions; he actually favors them over those with more universal meaning.

In fact, Yitzy has become a veritable signaling machine: in his world, an escalating parade of loyalty-affirming signals has crowded out the more intuitive and substantive aspects of tradition. For example, if in earlier times in the United States, avoiding non-kosher meat or processed foods containing non-kosher ingredients was sufficiently onerous to serve as an effective signal, the easy availability of kosher meat and snacks has rendered such signals insufficiently costly and hence ineffective. For Yitzy, the old standards of *kashrut* have been replaced by a steady parade of obscure stringencies climbing the ladder of costliness and strictness. Less benignly, when Yitzy signals his loyalty to the home team by burning bridges to the outside world through, for example, denying his children basic skills necessary for interacting with outsiders in a civil manner or earning a living, he is encouraging both boorishness and financial dependence on entitlements distributed by the very society of which he and his friends are trying to remain independent.

At the same time, Yitzy and his friends are cynical about even the positive aspects of Heidi's ambition for fairness, and this cynicism sometimes leads them to wink at moral violations, particularly in certain financial matters. There seems to be a kind of moral licensing going on here: when people feel they've discharged their moral duties more than adequately in one area, they allow themselves liberties in other areas. And, as some discover too late, those who tolerate delinquents just because they're on their team soon become their victims.

Finally, Yitzy is not merely punctilious about halakha, his whole conception of halakha and the way it is meant to be studied and practiced is different from Shimen's. Yitzy's yeshiva education emphasized book knowledge over mimetic tradition. As a result, the version of halakha that matters for him – not the one he learned at home, but the one he learned in yeshiva[1] – is over-codified to the point of counter-intuitiveness and often baroque in its pointless complexity. It is very much a second language, formal and sapped of vitality, and it saturates the mind with distracting detail.

* * *

If Yitzy does battle with Heidi by becoming her mirror image – she overvalues fairness and he undervalues it – his cousin Ben does battle with Heidi by lagging about a decade behind her.

---

1. Unlike in hasidic circles where influence is held by communal leaders, the most influential leaders in *yeshivish* circles are heads of talmudic academies, who tend to be somewhat detached from communal norms and concerns. In the United States, it is common for young men raised in hasidic families, like Yitzy, to attend non-hasidic yeshivas and to adopt the ivory-tower elitism characteristic of many of those institutions.

Ben remains a nominally observant Jew, but interacts with Heidi's world as a matter of course on a daily basis. He has internalized Heidi's cosmopolitan assumptions about the world far more than he realizes. He is just a bit uncomfortable with his community's provincial-seeming loyalties; he values tradition up to the point where it seriously impedes self-fulfillment; he privately regards observant Jews as holding immature and foolish beliefs about the world. He is culturally and politically a blue-state American, even if he is committed to the set of lifestyle constraints characteristic of his community.

Ben is a principled fellow. As he internalizes more of Heidi's values but remains formally committed to halakha, he feels like a hypocrite – a state of affairs for which he has an exaggerated distaste. His solution is to tweak halakha a bit, round a few edges, de-emphasize a few things and re-emphasize a few others.

I've got nothing against tweaks; Shimen took some liberties, too, and I regard that as a feature, not a bug. But Ben isn't Shimen. When Shimen's instincts ran up against the letter of the law, he knew just how far he could push, and he felt completely comfortable doing so. Shimen was sufficiently at home in halakha that such conflicts caused him no anxiety, and he was sufficiently respectful of halakha that he wouldn't think of tampering with it to reconcile it with what he chose to do. If that's hypocrisy, he was in favor of it.

Ben, however, is reconciling halakha with values that he has imbibed from outside of it, and he knows it. He's not confident enough just to push at the edges in his own practice while leaving halakha alone. He's exactly knowledgeable enough to dredge up and tendentiously interpret Jewish texts in a rather unpersuasive attempt to drag halakha in his preferred direction. The exercise is doomed to failure, because it involves chasing a moving target. So long as Heidi's world sits prominently in Ben's mental audience, his halakhic red lines will never lag more than a decade or so behind her progressive red lines.

Shimen would neither understand nor approve Ben's attempts at accommodation.

* * *

This, then, is how Yitzy and Ben grew apart. A free and open society like the United States tempts members of distinct subcultures to choose a primary audience; Yitzy chose the inside audience and Ben chose the outside audience. The choice of primary audience is the watershed; once it is decided, all else flows in a determined direction.

Yitzy and Ben are not simply on divergent paths; in fact, they drive each other further and further apart. Ben's slouching toward Heidi's world alerts Yitzy to the dangers of lowering the fences. As Yitzy raises the fences through conspicuous bridge-burning signals, Ben is both offended by what he regards as a debasement of Judaism and embarrassed, fearful that Yitzy's behavior will lower his own status in the eyes of outsiders. Furthermore, as Yitzy's community progressively devalues what Ben believes is his competitive advantage – the ability to bridge worlds – Ben seeks less affirmation from Yitzy's world. Increasingly, his primary audience is Heidi and her friends.

I don't want to overstate my case. Certainly, many American Jews – of various institutional affiliations – manage to perch themselves at the small plateau at the top of the ridge, skillfully balancing their commitments. The very best people who pray with Yitzy and the very best people who pray with Ben all carry on Shimen's legacy in an honorable way and remain as connected to each other as Yitzy and Ben were in their youth. Many of them have mastered the art of retaining strong Jewish identities, fidelity to tradition, and knowledge of Torah, even while advancing toward the pinnacle of American professional life.

And, yet, the ridge is narrow and unstable. Even the most well-integrated committed Jews in America live compartmentalized lives. They play successfully to two audiences, but never quite at the same time. Some of their kids remain on the ridge, but many become either Yitzies or Bens. For the most part, the Yitzies will produce more Yitzies behind ever higher walls and the Bens will produce Heidis who produce Ambers. None will produce Shimens.

I would like to believe that with time the Yitzies will become less cynical and formalistic and the Bens will become less acculturated and self-conscious. But I fear that nothing approximating Shimen's *Yiddishkeit* is likely to survive for long in America or anywhere else outside of Israel.

Chapter 15

Jewish Statism

Shimen was in many ways the ultimate *galuti* (diaspora) character. For Shimen, power meant nothing more than the ability to live his life according to his community's traditions and to pass on his cultural and intellectual legacy to his children. The capacity to move armies was not among his aspirations. He was suspicious of, if not downright antagonistic to, political authority.

The War changed Shimen's mind about the insignificance of political power. He understood well the cost of powerlessness and didn't wish to suffer its consequences again. Nevertheless, it wasn't important enough to him in the aftermath of The War to choose Israel over the United States. He claimed it was a matter of chance, boat schedules and the like, but I suspect he didn't have the stomach for the inevitable internal squabbling as Jews came to terms with their own sovereignty. Shimen didn't want power; he wanted peace and quiet.

So, it would be no small irony if some version of his form of *Yiddishkeit* were ultimately to be revived specifically in Israel.

But is such a revival of organic Judaism in Israel really in the cards? After all, if American Jews have failed to balance universal and particularist values (as discussed in Part 1), have not Israeli Jews failed to balance state power and traditional communal norms (as discussed in Part 2)? In this chapter, I'll offer the reasons to be pessimistic; in the next chapter, I'll offer the reasons to be optimistic.

Heidi, Yitzy, and Ben can be understood only in the context of American culture and the challenges that culture presents to Jews as a minority in the United States. To highlight the ways in which the Israeli experience has been different from the American one, we'll introduce in this chapter the Israeli counterparts of Heidi, Yitzy, and Ben: Adi, Itcha Meir, and Bentzi. Before we get to them, we'll provide some historical background on the situation in Israel through the character of Yossel, a member of Shimen's generation, who chose a different path than Shimen. The character sketches presented here, like those of Yitzy and Ben above, will necessarily be briefer and less finely drawn than those of Shimen and Heidi, but I'm hopeful that the narrative benefits of introducing these characters will outweigh the cost of stereotyping them.

YOSSEL THE RENEGADE ZIONIST

Shimen's childhood friend Yossel grew up in a family of Gerer Hasidim in the Polish town of Dvort, near Lodz. After his bar mitzva, he and Shimen studied Torah together in the study hall presided over by the famed scholar Rabbi Meir Dan Plotzky (d. 1928). Yossel was regarded as a promising talmudic scholar, but, like many of his friends, he felt stifled by the lack of economic and intellectual opportunity in his provincial town and social milieu. At the age of sixteen, he left for the more metropolitan Warsaw, where he abandoned the hasidic way of life and eventually took up the study of law. Unlike many of his friends who had traveled a similar path, he did not join the anti-Zionist Jewish-socialist Bund party, but rather became active in Al Hamishmar, a radical pro-Zionist party with representation in the Polish Sejm that opposed anti-Semitism and hasidic Judaism with approximately equal fervor.

In 1935, Yossel left for the Land of Israel, joining Kibbutz Beit Alfa. Educated and clever, and not cut out for manual labor, he quickly became active in the politics of the kibbutz movement, taking a leading role in moving Beit Alfa from its affiliation with the socialist Mapai to the more hard-core communist Mapam.

Yossel's Zionism was rooted in the understanding that the Jews had no future in Poland and that without a state of their own, they had no future anywhere. But for him and his friends, Zionism was about much more than just self-defense; they sought nothing less than the transformation of the Jewish psyche. In the years leading up to the foundation of the state, Yossel anticipated that statehood would force the Jews to overcome old habits of quietism and forbearance and to replace the authority of elders and sages with the authority of the young and vital. He hoped the state would become an arbiter and enforcer of new values and would use its authority to promote ideas and norms central to the secular nationalist ethos.

In his enthusiasm, Yossel failed to grasp that a Jewish nationalism stripped of the traditions that defined the Jewish nation would lead to policies riddled with self-contradiction. True, in the aftermath of the foundation of the state, his nationalism was such that he welcomed to Israel Jewish immigrants from deeply traditional backgrounds, despite the immense cost of absorbing them. But, in the absence of shared beliefs and practices, he could not quite develop genuine empathy for these helpless newcomers. He was thus entirely sympathetic to state policies in which traditional Sephardic immigrants were dumped, against their will, in distant development towns and their children were indoctrinated in secular kibbutzim like his own Beit Alfa, with the intention of transforming "human dust into a cultured nation," as David Ben-Gurion put it.

As for Yossel's few surviving childhood friends who came to Israel after The War, he regarded them with a certain degree of contempt for their weakness; they, in turn, were ashamed to speak of their experiences. By contrast, his friend Shimen, who did not go to Israel after The War, was most certainly not ashamed to speak of his experiences. On the one occasion he visited Israel, he and Yossel argued bitterly. Shimen insisted that there was heroism in maintaining one's dignity and faith in the face of terrible suffering, and Yossel was just as insistent that dying helplessly in a concentration camp could never constitute dignity or justify faith.[1]

Shimen was disgusted that Yossel supported the state's decision to commemorate The War by emphasizing the Warsaw Ghetto uprising, as if the mere murder of six million Jews were an embarrassment unworthy of commemoration for its own sake. Yossel told Shimen straightforwardly that his choice of the United States over Israel was a display of unforgivable weakness and escapism.

Despite his secularism, Yossel saw in Zionism elements of the biblical narrative and viewed the return of the Jews to Israel in millennial terms. But his millennialism derived more from Hegel's romantic nationalism and Marx's dialectical materialism than from the prophecies of Isaiah. Similarly, Yossel's ideological collectivism required that the Jewish state supersede Jewish communities. He wished to replace traditional religion with socialism and communal social norms with state laws.

Yossel's contempt for traditional Jewish communities was, to say the least, not a promising foundation for the revival of organic Judaism. As I've explained in Chapter 8, the regulatory welfare state cannot replace moral communities. Its top-down structure fails to incorporate the moral intuitions of its members

---

1. The substance of their argument is captured well in the 1951 Yiddish short story by Chaim Grade, "*Mayn krig mit Hersh Raseyner*" [My Quarrel with Hersh Rasseyner], which first appeared in English in the anthology, Irving Howe and Eliezer Greenberg, *A Treasury of Yiddish Stories* (New York: Viking Press, 1954).

and its attempts at social engineering are doomed to backfire. But, for Yossel and other escapees from the shtetl, religion and free markets were evils that needed to be overcome and the state was the vehicle for overcoming them. The result is that Yossel and his fellow collectivists who wished to liberate themselves from the tyranny of rabbis instead subjected multiple generations in Israel to the tyranny of bureaucrats.

On the face of it, none of this should augur well for a revival of Shimen's version of communal Judaism in Israel. Simply put, organic Judaism cannot take root among those whose primary identity is Israeli rather than Jewish. If this were true for Yossel's generation, it is even more so for the generations after Yossel.

ADI THE BLUE-BLOODED JURIST

Yossel's son Haimke attended Hebrew University's law school in the early 1960s, rising up to become a prominent member of the first generation of Israeli-born judges. He shared his father's secular, socialist Zionist views, though he was less resentful of old-fashioned Judaism than was his formerly religious father. Haimke regarded religious Judaism as a mere relic that could be benignly ignored as it suffered inelegantly through its death throes. A proud and active member of Israel's dominant Mapai Party until he joined the bench, Haimke always felt that he had deservedly earned his place among Israel's ruling elite. To his dying day, Haimke regarded the Likud Party's defeat of Mapai in the 1977 Israeli elections, as well as the rule of various subsequent capitalist-reactionary governments, as historical accidents destined to be reversed in due time.

Haimke's daughter Adi, who will serve here as an Israeli counterpart to Heidi, followed in her father's footsteps, studying philosophy and law at Hebrew University in the 1980s. Adi shares many of the views of her father and grandfather, though she is somewhat perplexed by their nationalism and has no patience for the once-fashionable Israeli male swagger. Judaism has no religious meaning for her, and she has become ambivalent about Jewish ethnicity; much more than Yossel and Haimke, she is an Israeli before she is a Jew. This creates significant dissonance for her regarding Israel's definition as a Jewish nation-state; when necessary, she pays lip service to the idea of a Jewish nation-state but feels uncomfortable with any of its manifestations. She has trouble justifying the Law of Return, regards singing "Hatikva" or displaying the Israeli flag as jingoistic, and is put off by overtly Jewish imagery.

She wishes that Israel be distinguished less by any specific Jewish character than by an embrace of the principles of international human-rights law, in return for which, she has no doubt, the world would welcome Israel as an equal and honored member of the family of nations. She believes that, regardless of the consequences for Israel's security, Israel is in violation of human-rights law as long as it does not withdraw every last Jew from the territory on which a Palestinian nation-state – with its own anthem, flag, and repatriation laws – must be established.

Unlike her American contemporary, Heidi, whose sympathy with the huddled masses is rooted in her own identity as a minority and grandchild of refugees, Adi thinks of herself as an Israeli blueblood, a descendant of prominent founding fathers. She seems unperturbed by the fact that her pedigree is rooted in the efforts of her father and grandfather to establish and strengthen an ethnic Jewish nation-state, the very idea of which makes her squirm. She prefers to think of herself as a member of a transnational community of progressive cosmopolitans, working selflessly in pursuit of progress and justice in the little backwater in which she happens to have been born.

Adi is deeply concerned about religious fundamentalists gaining political strength and confidence. Unlike her father, who regarded the rise of the Israeli Right as a passing phase, Adi regards it as a long-term threat to Israel's soul, if not to its very existence. Adi is convinced that certain elements of Israeli society have designs on political power that they have not earned; they have not undergone the ideological and psychological transitions required for political leadership, from traditional Jewish *galuti* modes of thought. They remain, in Adi's view, mired in messianic, unproductive, and sectorial ways of thinking, and do not sufficiently understand the principles of democracy.

Adi believes that the hawkish views of Israeli religious rightwingers are rooted in a fanatical and unfounded belief in divine providence. She herself has been active in Peace Now her entire adult life; she believes that were it not for the messianic predilections of her political opponents, Israelis would have long ago been vacationing on the shores of Beirut and eating hummus in the bazaars of Damascus.

Adi also resents the religious communities for not sufficiently appreciating the role of modernity and enlightenment values in promoting prosperity and driving productivity. Due to their limited secular education, members of these communities aspire at most to be merchants and tradesmen, while Adi and her friends studied Marcuse and Althusser in university and go on to important public-sector jobs.

Adi also regards religious people as being excessively clannish and focusing on narrow sectorial interests, lacking the social maturity to see the big picture. Appreciating the importance of having people with the right views making policy, Adi has sacrificed opportunities in the private sector to practice public law. With only a bit of help from her well-connected father, Adi landed a job as a junior attorney in the Attorney General's office, and she has been rising through the ranks there ever since.

Adi is devoted to the protection of her own particular version of democracy. She fully believes that the religious are in thrall to a powerful cadre of rabbis who hold what she regards as primitive views on modern society and who have limited respect for the legal bureaucracy. Recognizing the threat to democracy posed by the rapid demographic growth of such people, Adi has become a prominent member of a powerful cadre of civil servants who serve as legal "gatekeepers" in the service of democracy, the main task of whom is preventing ideologically problematic elected officials from governing according to their whims.

Adi's clout lies not only in the authority she and her colleagues have taken for themselves but in their ability to project an image of enlightened power-wielding. She revels in the fact that ambitious legal eagles and aspiring intellectuals, especially those whose natural political and religious milieu would not ordinarily align them with Adi and her friends, have long since figured out which opinions must be parroted and whose vanity must be flattered, if they wish to get ahead.

Shimen at least enjoyed arguing with Adi's grandfather Yossel, but I suspect that Shimen wouldn't much enjoy arguing with Adi. It's not just that, unlike Yossel, she's ignorant on matters of Judaism and lacking in loyalty to the Jewish people; she also seems to lack self-awareness and a sense of irony.

ITCHA MEIR AND BENTZI

If traditional Jews in America, like Yitzy and Ben, split over how to deal with the challenge posed by Heidi, traditional Jews in Israel split over how to deal with the challenge posed by her counterpart, Adi. Consider now the Israeli counterparts of Yitzy and Ben: Itcha Meir and Bentzi. Like their American doppelgangers, Itcha Meir and Bentzi are cousins born to Polish survivors in the 1960s. Like Yitzy and Ben, they have drifted far apart, but the principal differences between Itcha Meir and Bentzi lie along a different dimension than those of Yitzy and Ben. While Itcha Meir and Bentzi do differ on matters of religious observance, they are distinguished mainly by their respective attitudes toward a Jewish state that, to a great extent, reflects the secular sensibilities of Yossel and Adi.

Itcha Meir's parents met in Israel in the late 1950s. Itcha Meir's father, Leibel, made a modest living as a watchmaker. Leibel was active in Poalei Agudah, a somewhat more Zionist affiliate of the *ḥaredi* non-Zionist Agudat Yisrael party, mainly because of a family connection to its leader, Binyomin Mintz. Although deeply suspicious of secular Zionists like Yossel, he was grateful that Jews could build and defend their own country and even volunteered briefly with the Israeli army in its earliest days. Leibel felt close to the Gerer Rebbe but tried to keep a safe distance. He steered clear of ideology and expected his oldest son, Itcha Meir, to share his sympathetic ambivalence toward Zionism.

Itcha Meir attended an elementary school where religious subjects were studied for most of the day but a few hours in the afternoon were devoted to secular subjects; on Shabbat afternoons, he attended youth groups run by Ezra, a religious Zionist youth movement slightly more old-fashioned on religious matters than the national-religious Bnei Akiva youth movement. But when the Gerer *yeshiva ketana* (high school focusing exclusively on Torah studies) opened its new building not far from Itcha Meir's home, the rebbe prevailed upon Leibel to let Itcha Meir study there rather than at a religious high school that included secular studies in the curriculum. Having internalized his father's soft spot for Hasidism, Itcha Meir adapted very quickly to his new yeshiva. He had already developed proficiency in the study of Talmud with commentaries and was pleased to devote himself to such study with greater intensity. He happily wore the standard outfit, a *bekeshe* and pants tucked into his socks (and even a specified type of underwear), and lived by all the yeshiva's very long list of rules, most of which involved avoiding women.

The view of the world that Itcha Meir imbibed in his years in the Gerer *yeshiva ketana* has stayed with him to this day, especially regarding Zionism. The yeshiva was aggressively anti-Zionist. Unlike many hasidic communities that originated in Hungary, the

Gerer yeshiva did not promote the view that Zionism was literally the work of Satan, but merely that it was conceptually misguided and substantively anti-religious. For the Gerers, Zionists like Yossel, who shifted the focus of Jewish peoplehood from shared religious obligations to a shared secular state, undermined the unity of the Jewish people. In their view, the Zionist redefinition of Jewish power from spiritual resistance to military strength weakened Judaism. On the practical level, they saw Zionist attempts to re-educate religious immigrants against their will as an affront to both Judaism and human decency. Itcha Meir found all this persuasive then and still does today.

But Itcha Meir's rejection of Zionism is not rooted so much in ideology as in a deep sense of alienation. Soldiering and performing physical labor seem to him to be the sorts of activities that *goyim*, non-Jews, ought to be doing, not nice Jewish boys. Exhibiting the same combination of elitism and naivete that characterizes graduate students everywhere, Itcha Meir simply pretends that security and industry materialize from the ether. In a similar vein, since the hasidic folklore to which he is greatly attached assumes a world in which Jews valiantly resist and outfox hostile *goyim*, Itcha Meir casts non-*haredi* Jews in Israel, especially secular bluebloods like Adi, in the role of the *goyim*. He speaks of "evil decrees" propagated by the regime against innocent *haredim*, such as slashing government funding of yeshivas, that "even the Polish government never dared do." One of Itcha Meir's more cynical Gerer friends is fond of pointing out to him that he is absolutely right: the Polish government never once cut subsidies to yeshivas.

Not serving in the Israeli army was a perfect bridge-burning signal for Itcha Meir in his youth, as it is now for his children. It significantly reduces their options outside the *haredi* world and hence reliably signals their loyalty to the community. But, unlike, for example, signaling loyalty by committing to costly stringencies regarding *kashrut*, draft avoidance is also costly to third parties.

For all of Shimen's disagreements with his secular Zionist friend Yossel, he had little patience for the assertive anti-Zionism of Itcha Meir's generation of Israeli Gerer Hasidim. He found their ideological arguments to be self-servingly disingenuous and to display what he regarded as an inexcusable lack of gratitude. He couldn't fathom how they could draw any kind of analogy between anti-Semitic Polish *goyim* and their own cousins in Israel; he found this kind of shallow reduction of a radically new situation to an old and familiar one to be both lazy and childish.

* * *

Itcha Meir isn't quite a modern-day version of Shimen, but neither is Itcha Meir's cousin, the religious-Zionist Bentzi. Bentzi grew up in Jerusalem and went to a yeshiva high school run by students of Rabbi Zvi Yehuda Kook. Rabbi Zvi Yehuda was the son of Rabbi Avraham Yitzhak Kook, father of the ideology that dominated religious Zionist educational institutions in Israel during Bentzi's school days in the 1970s. After high school, Bentzi attended a *hesder* yeshiva, where he alternated between yeshiva studies and army service. Bentzi was so taken with the anti-*galuti* spirit of his yeshiva that, for example, he had no interest in joining his father's annual nostalgia visits to the Gerer Rebbe.

Bentzi and Itcha Meir have never been especially close, but when they meet at family celebrations, Bentzi knows just how to get Itcha Meir's goat. He provokes an argument about *ḥaredi* draft evasion and then seizes on the contradiction between Itcha Meir's two lines of counter-attack. Sometimes Itcha Meir's claim is that Zionism is a fundamentally secular movement with which Itcha Meir and his family do not identify, and they can't be expected to fight its wars. But on other occasions, Itcha Meir's claim is that precisely because Israel is a Jewish state, its government should recognize the important contribution of Torah scholars to the spiritual well-being of the Jewish people and hence willingly grant them a dispensation. Every time they get to this point in the conversation, Bentzi gestures with his thumb and shouts "*Nu, mima nafshakh!*" which is the technical talmudic term for "Either way, your argument is flawed."

Still, for all his arguments with Itcha Meir, Bentzi has a somewhat greater connection to *haredim* like Itcha Meir than to secularists like Yossel and Adi. If Yossel and, to a lesser extent, Adi are committed to some version of Zionism but not to Torah, and Itcha Meir is committed to Torah but not to Zionism, Bentzi and his friends are committed to both Torah and Zionism. They study the same Torah as *haredim* and do national service like secular Zionists. Bentzi is convinced that as such they could serve as a bridge between the world of Yossel and Adi and that of Itcha Meir. He has never himself quite grasped why nobody has ever shown any interest in buying the bridge he's been selling. But the explanation is actually quite straightforward and is also the key to understanding why Shimen wouldn't feel at home in Bentzi's world.

Bentzi's version of religious Zionism is not intermediate between secular Zionism and religious non-Zionism; more specifically, it is not merely the union of Zionism and religious Judaism. Rather, as followers of Rabbi Kook (Kookniks, for short) have always stressed, religious-Zionism is a new hyphenated ideology in which statism is reinterpreted in religious terms and Judaism takes on a statist character. For Yossel and Adi, statism has to replace religion; for Itcha Meir, religion has to reject statism. But for Bentzi and his fellow Kookniks, the renewal of Jewish statism is the very heart of a religious redemptive process.

As an enthusiastic adherent of the Kookian view, Bentzi embraces the new definition of national power. He regards the tools of state-building – agriculture, military, industry – not simply as necessary burdens but as sacred endeavors worthy of the kind of veneration once reserved for matters of the spirit: army uniforms are for him the new "priestly garments." For Bentzi, Gerer political subversiveness has been replaced by its polar opposite, *mamlakh-tiut*, the doctrine that whatever apparent flaws the state and its institutions might suffer from, they and their proximate agents should be regarded as endowed with a divine imprimatur. Moreover, for Bentzi the state is the appropriate authority for deciding and regulating religious matters: the state ought to appoint rabbis, enforce religious legislation, and fund religious services. The replacement of religious community organizations with state institutions is the fulfillment of God's promise of *"ve'ashiva shoftayikh kevarishona,"* "I shall restore your judges as once were" (Isaiah 1:26), so that even secular officials, by virtue of being agents of the state and hence the bearers of profound unconscious religious longings, can be trusted to manage religious affairs.

As a hard-bitten realist, Shimen could not identify with any of this. Having suffered the consequences of statelessness, he was grateful for a powerful Jewish state, with all its flaws. He would see no value in Bentzi's conjuring a virtual idealized state, devoid of any resemblance to the actual imperfect state on the ground, and declaring it *yesod kisei Hashem ba'olam* ("the foundation of God's seat in the world," a phrase coined by the elder Rabbi Kook). Such fantasies have consequences, none of them good.

Only in Bentzi's virtual idealized state would it be a plausible idea to entrust bureaucrats with the management of religious affairs. Shimen could never imagine, for example, what good could come from a rabbi being appointed to a community by distant government bureaucrats, probably on the basis of patronage. For Shimen, a rabbi was simply someone who had earned respect from a community for his Torah scholarship, leadership, and moral stature; he had no use for someone handed the title of community rabbi and paid a salary by the state. He agreed with the cynical premise underlying the suggestion of the philosopher David Hume with regard to clergy that the government ought "to bribe their indolence, by assigning stated salaries to their profession, and rendering it superfluous for them to be farther active than merely to prevent their flock from straying in quest of new pastures."[2] As government-supported civil servants unaccountable to their communities but vulnerable to pressure by state officials and to second-guessing by the courts, official rabbis have the wrong incentives.

Furthermore, as someone familiar with disillusionment, Shimen well understood that the kind of enthusiastic and naive utopianism that burdens the state with unrealistic expectations is bound to backfire. Shimen would not be in the least surprised to learn that in addition to being over-represented among the ranks of combat officers, graduates of religious Zionist institutions are disproportionately involved in the leadership of radical Israeli organizations devoted, in the name of universal brotherhood and cosmic justice, to securing the interests of those who wish the Jews dead and their state destroyed. Disappointed idealists are prone to trading one messianic fantasy for another.

In short, Shimen would not recognize any of the naturalness or authenticity of his own Judaism in the worlds of Adi, Itcha Meir, or Bentzi.

So, can anything resembling Shimen's organic Judaism emerge from this unlikely trio, or are they all hopelessly trapped in their positions? I'll dangle a clue: Bentzi's ideology, like the mustache he still sports un-ironically, is beginning to look dated even within his own community. Itcha Meir's community is growing tired of its self-imposed poverty. And Adi's kids find her snobbishness embarrassing.

---

2. David Hume, *History of England*, chapter 29 (Indianapolis, IN: Liberty Classics, 1762, 1983).

Chapter 16

The Revival of Organic Judaism

It seems there are plenty of ways to get Judaism wrong. The two American cousins, Yitzy and Ben (and, truth be told, many of Shimen's contemporaries between the two world wars), challenged by the openness of Heidi's world and educated to defensiveness, were not able to keep the system in equilibrium. Yitzy never developed healthy moral intuitions and hence lacks the confidence to contribute to shaping the soft edges of halakha. His Judaism is formalistic; it's weak on the universal component and doesn't adapt well. Similarly, Ben never developed a sufficiently thorough body of halakhic knowledge or appreciation of the wisdom of the ages. His Judaism is shallow; it's weak on the particularist component and is not very stable; he is acculturating faster than he realizes.

The two Israeli cousins, Itcha Meir and Bentzi, challenged by statist enthusiasm, have faltered as well. Bentzi's Judaism has become somewhat politicized and lifeless as he unwittingly weakens Jewish communities by supporting the state's usurpation of their roles. Itcha Meir's Judaism has become cynical due to his refusal to acknowledge how the existence of such a state changes the nature of the challenges faced by Jewish tradition.

As for our two secularists, they are more similar than they know. Adi's anti-religious post-nationalist culture, like Heidi's, holds no promise as a foundation for a new version of Judaism and possesses dim prospects as a flourishing culture of any sort.

In short, there is nothing in our cast of characters' respective versions of Judaism that would put one in mind of a project connecting a richly recalled past with an intensely conceived future, giving life direction and meaning. What grounds, then, are there for believing that there is hope for traditional Judaism to return to some state of equilibrium? The prospect that Shimen's formative life experiences – hasidic life in the shtetl, suffering in the camps and the murder of his family and friends, adaptation to a new and cosmopolitan world – will be reproduced on any scale in the near-term is as unlikely as it is unwelcome. From where then might there emerge new Shimens with the requisite knowledge and moral intuition, humility and confidence, and rootedness in the past and trust in the future to revive a viable version of Judaism?

BOXES

The key to the problem might be that all our characters, both the American and Israeli trios, seem to live in boxes. The circumstances of their lives are such that the range of realizable positions along the continuum of Jewish identity and practice is limited to a small set of available boxes. These boxes – secular-cosmopolitan, modern-religious, *ḥaredi*, or whatever – are hard to avoid or escape due to the necessity for signaling games and wagon-circling in hostile intellectual environments. These boxes are characterized by ideological least common denominators, fusty institutional interests, and intellectual conformity.

But American and Israeli Jews are not equally encumbered by the extent to which their Jewishness is boxed.

A generation ago, in the days when I was being lectured on Jewish duties by Heidi in Princeton, it would have been clear that Israel was much boxier than the United States. Shimen and the parents of Yitzy and Ben sat so comfortably between the *ḥaredi* and Modern Orthodox worlds that they were completely unaware that the distinction even mattered. Similarly, the Conservative community in which Heidi grew up filled the gap between Modern Orthodoxy and secular cosmopolitanism.

In Israel, on the other hand, the gap between anti-religious secularists like Adi and religious Zionists like Bentzi was occupied solely by marginalized traditional Sephardim, who had yet to find a strong and distinctive voice. The split between Bentzi and Itcha Meir caused by their different attitudes toward participation in military service led to other dichotomies: most religious Zionists entered the job market at an age when Itcha Meir's friends had to remain in yeshiva to evade the draft. American Jews who moved to Israel were often frustrated by the unavailability of the kinds of intermediate versions of Jewishness to which they were accustomed.

Some of this still holds to a lesser degree, but if instead of looking at snapshots of Judaism in the United States and in Israel, we consider the respective trajectories of developments in each country since those days, a different picture emerges.

Judaism in the United States has become much boxier. Just as Israeli young men have to choose between serving in the army or avoiding the draft, young American Jews need to decide between remaining in the ghetto or buying into the dominant campus culture – Heidi's cosmopolitanism, if they're lucky, or Amber's radicalism, if they're not. The social and professional cost of bucking that trend is quite high and is only worthwhile in exchange for the social capital available exclusively in very tight-knit and isolated Jewish communities.

The fate of the Conservative congregation in which Heidi grew up is instructive in this regard. In trying to cater to Heidi's cohort, the congregation briefly resisted but then enthusiastically adopted every fashionable progressive trend until it was left with no distinctive message to offer. Broadly speaking, the offspring of Heidi's friends – to the extent that they have any – are, like Amber, less Jewish and more radical than their parents. The congregation's building was recently sold to a Korean church.

As it happens, Ben's kids and Yitzy's kids are also drifting further from their grandparents' delicate balance. Of Ben's three children, one son is no longer affiliated with a Jewish community and another is a member of a Reconstructionist LGBT community; Ben's daughter has gone *yeshivish* and lives in the religious Jerusalem neighborhood of Ramat Eshkol with her husband, who shares her background and is now, as he would put it in his newly adopted *yeshivish* English, "learning by Reb Avrohom Yehoshua," referring to the famously stern leader of a rather hard-core yeshiva, hoping (vainly) that the head of the yeshiva will one day nod in his general direction.

Yitzy has three daughters and three sons, in that order. He believes he hit the jackpot with his eldest daughter's husband by promising to forgo retirement to support his daughter's family while his son-in-law sits in *kollel* (a yeshiva for married students) for the rest of his life. He could not afford a similar arrangement for his second daughter and had to settle for a lesser scholar; his third daughter is having trouble finding a match altogether. As for his sons, the younger two are both studying in yeshiva; the older of the two is seeking a father-in-law who will help him to continue studying in yeshiva indefinitely, while the youngest is secretly planning to one day make a killing in real estate. Yitzy's eldest son, once the apple of his eye, is now never spoken of, so as not to harm the others' chances of getting good matches; he had been serially molested by his fourth-grade instructor in Jewish texts and is addicted to opioids and no longer religiously observant. Yitzy's daughters are decently educated and hard-working; his sons and sons-in-law speak English, Yiddish, and Hebrew, but might be hard-pressed to complete a sentence in any of the three. Except for Ben's *yeshivish* daughter who seeks out the company of her second cousins, Ben's kids and Yitzy's kids each regard the other as object lessons in the dangers of the wrong kind of Jewish education and want nothing to do with each other. Their estrangement is representative of the broader bad relationship into which some of their respective cohorts have been sucked, one characterized by mistrust, spite, and alienation.

* * *

Those who don't follow closely might be surprised to hear that the current situation in Israel is quite different. Israel has become much less "boxy." The default culture is no longer that of secular progressives like Adi, and there is now little pressure to conform to it. Unlike in the United States, the threat of assimilation is limited, so the degree of fear across groups is diminishing. Moreover, the rigid ideologies that separate Israeli *haredim*, religious Zionists, and secular progressives are becoming increasingly irrelevant.

Itcha Meir's kids are Gerer Hasidim like him, but they speak standard Hebrew; their political views are Zionist in substance even if not in name; and they would love to find a way to learn a trade and make an honest living. Bentzi's kids got the full Kooknik education, but they have lived through the Oslo Agreements, the Disengagement, and other follies of Israeli governments and openly mock their father's Kookian ideology as detached from reality. Adi's kids – even the secular Adi has a Jewish husband and three kids – are embarrassed at their parents' firm, if unspoken, conviction that the state is rightly owned by the descendants of Mapai bluebloods and that others live here at their sufferance.

Two of the three are married to descendants of immigrants from Islamic countries, who share neither the anti-traditionalism nor the elitism of Adi's Ashkenazic family.

Adi's kids and Bentzi's kids meet in the army and at work, and they speak to each other with typical Israeli candidness, free of both rancor and the kind of correctness that typically stems from distance or mistrust. Increasingly, Itcha Meir's kids are participating in these conversations as well; once a practical solution is found to the problem of *ḥaredi* enlistment, the gap between them and the others will close at an accelerated pace.

In short, the boxes are breaking down in Israel. The question "Are you secular or religious or *ḥaredi*?" is, for many Israelis, becoming hard to answer. Increasingly, degrees of Jewish observance in Israel lie on a spectrum, not in the familiar boxes, gradually moving toward a normal distribution over the range, with a peak somewhere in the center that drops off slowly and symmetrically. As a result, there are long tails on each end populated by loud and strident outliers that give the impression that extremists are getting stronger, but this is an illusion.

Stereotypes are unraveling. We have become accustomed to the idea that if we know how someone dresses or how they behave in a given situation or where they studied, we can pretty much guess all the rest. Forget that. The flourishing of a Jewish state and the confidence it has brought are leading to a new and surprising realignment.

Let's consider now the nature of this realignment, what it tells us about the actual, and much misunderstood, value of a Jewish state, and how all this heralds the return of an organic Judaism last seen in the days of Shimen.

JUDAISM AS MAJORITY CULTURE

Most of the people who hang around in my think tank in Jerusalem are in their 20s and 30s. One grew up in a hasidic family with a father like Itcha Meir but now self-defines as non-religious and is beginning an academic career. One woman grew up in a non-observant family and was active in the peace movement and is now religiously observant and an expert on and sympathizer with the hard-core of the settlement movement. Another woman grew up in a traditional Sephardic family and remains unself-consciously traditional while writing a doctoral thesis on the transmission of religious folklore. One fellow was raised in a secular-Zionist family with a mom like Adi and still self-defines as non-religious, but he prays with a *minyan* every day and observes Shabbat. Another was raised in a scrupulously religious family and remains observant, but, as a matter of principle, he refuses to cover his head with a *kippa*. One fellow is a product of Kookian religious Zionism with a dad like Bentzi, but is now a gung-ho evangelist for full-throated capitalism. Another just completed a thesis on the phenomenon of Israeli celebrities, mostly artists and musicians, who are now loosely connected to various Jewish spiritual groups, most prominently Breslov, and are observant in a variety of idiosyncratic ways, but refuse to self-define as either religious or non-religious.

You might find any one of these life choices laudable or lamentable, but that's not the point. The phenomenon is interesting in aggregate. There seems to be a great deal of fluidity here, and the fluidity is strangely painless. These people are comfortable with themselves and with each other. What's this all about?

We've grown so accustomed to the centrality of signaling in Judaism that we can hardly imagine what Judaism would be like with less of it. We wear *shtreimlekh* or hats or *kippot* of a certain color or none of the above, we pray in this synagogue but never in that one, we use the right dialect of Yinglish and the appropriate accent, we eat here but not there, we flaunt our very special family customs, we bagel, we *batel*, we battle. We are so used to Judaism being spoken like a second language that we are perplexed when we see the early signs of the return of Judaism as a first language.

Young Israelis like the men and women in my office and the sons and daughters of Itcha Meir, Bentzi, and Adi, aspire for Judaism to be a culture, not a counter-culture. They don't need to prove they're not assimilating; there aren't enough non-Jews here to assimilate into (which is why Itcha Meir, unlike his kids, needs to imagine Zionists as "*goyim*" just to keep his shtick going). They have no interest in wasting energy on broadcasting their loyalty to this box and not that box. That mix-and-match of modes of dress, outlook, and practice that seems incongruous to old fogies and diaspora Jews are simply inchoate attempts at breaking down the boxes and separating the signals from the substance. Shimen was an old fogy and a diaspora Jew and I'm quite certain he wouldn't have quite "gotten" these young people, but I'd like to believe that he'd have recognized in them some of the authenticity and the vitality that he had seen destroyed and feared lost.

Adi, Bentzi, Itcha Meir, and their friends could very well be the last of the ideological dinosaurs. Many members of the generation after them are looking for some form of authentic Judaism rich enough, substantial enough, realistic enough to serve as a national culture and not merely as a counter-culture sufficient to sustain a minority. If I might borrow a business term, they are looking for a version of Judaism that scales. This will happen slowly and from the bottom up; it will involve dead ends, intellectual fads, and ill-considered compromises. But the trend is positive.

Already there are some small, tentative steps in interesting directions. Galgalatz, the radio station that determines Israel's Top 40 hits, includes in its playlist songs that break down all the boundaries between secular and religious music, seamlessly combining eastern and western religious liturgy with contemporary folk and rock styles. Literary awards go to books that straddle the boundary between secular and religious literature in a fashion reminiscent of that of Israel's first Nobel laureate, S. Y. Agnon. Safed and Jerusalem are flush with galleries purveying serious (and not serious) contemporary art with profounder Jewish content than Chagall. This isn't much, but it's a start.

* * *

A much bigger question is what is happening with halakha.

Halakha can't and shouldn't change dramatically and quickly for all the reasons I explained in Part 2. But circumstances change, sometimes dramatically, and halakha can either adapt to new circumstances in ways that preserve its underlying principles and experiential resonance or it can be reduced to mere formalism. Consider some examples of halakhic developments in the face of industrialization and technological innovation and possible further such developments in the face of anticipated technological innovation.

In households like Shimen's in the shtetl in Poland, *kashrut* involved taking a chicken to a qualified *shoḥet* (ritual slaughterer), checking the slaughtered chicken for significant imperfections, soaking and salting the meat, draining blood from the liver over an open flame, and other such ritual preparations. Shimen's community didn't abstain from occasionally eating meat, which made them ever conscious that their moral obligations to humans were greater than those to animals, but these arduous rituals made eating meat an act undertaken with full awareness that an animal's life had been taken for one's benefit – not unlike today's "kill what you eat" movement. For moderns, *kashrut* means little more than looking for the right symbol on the package in the freezer section; this simplicity is a convenience, but it dims the intended awareness. Once synthetic meat becomes sufficiently convincing and affordable, the laws of *kashrut* might find some new meaning, or they might, as real meat falls out of common use, become largely irrelevant – for better or for worse.

Similarly, Shabbat in modern urban areas, especially in the era of modern heating and lighting systems and automatic timers, is not quite the same retreat from the workaday world that it once was for Shimen in the shtetl. Once self-driving vehicles and ubiquitous digital devices are commonplace, the rules of Shabbat might become too easily circumvented via automation, or alternatively, they could become an inhospitable prison. But, if the right balance is struck, Shabbat rules could serve as a well-calibrated solution to the psychological and social challenges associated with relentless connectivity and distraction.

Some of the most far-reaching changes to life as we know it are likely to result from the near-elimination of transaction costs for most financial interactions.[1] Online markets eliminate the cost of establishing trust and of matching buyers and sellers, while related technologies, including self-driving vehicles, will eventually greatly reduce the cost of delivery. As a result, most of the things we own today – houses, cars, appliances, and more – will be shared in various ways that radically alter the very notion of ownership as we currently understand it. Halakha has lagged in adapting to constructions as commonplace as limited liability companies and intellectual property. Will it deal successfully with radically new conceptions of ownership and transaction?

The decreased need for human labor is likely to result in some form of universal basic income and to greatly increase leisure time for almost everyone, for better or worse. Jewish norms of charity could become outdated and inapt, or they could adapt and find new application. The Jewish ideal of using all available time

---

1. Mike Munger, *Tomorrow 3.0: Transaction Costs and the Sharing Economy* (Cambridge, UK: Cambridge University Press, 2018).

for study could be dumbed down by a society of the chronically under-employed or it could become a model for the constructive and satisfying use of leisure time.

Programming self-driving vehicles (as you can see, a favorite topic of mine) requires coding decisions for situations substantively identical to the trolley problems we considered in Chapter 7. Rabbinic literature, such as the Ḥazon Ish discussion referenced there, includes thoughtful consideration of such problems. This literature might remain esoteric and theoretical, or it might serve as the basis for more sophisticated discussions germane to the kinds of challenges that new technologies introduce.

Perhaps most dramatically, advances in biotechnology are already beginning to raise questions regarding the nature of maternity and paternity and even life and death, while genetic and digital modification of species will inevitably raise questions regarding the nature of humanity. Halakha could contribute a serious and sober long view on such matters, rooted in millennia of thoughtful engagement with fundamental questions, or it could prove to be sterile, formalistic, and irrelevant.

It would be foolhardy to try to anticipate how halakha will adapt to each of these challenges and to many more I haven't mentioned or even thought of. I can only put forth two claims with some degree of confidence. First, that different communities will try different paths, and that some of them will adapt and survive and others will fail to adapt and wither. Second, that in Israel, the adaptations will reflect the situation in which Jews are a majority exercising a large degree of political and cultural autonomy.

There is a difference, for example, between Shabbat as a personal observance and Shabbat as a communal, and even national, day of rest, prayer, and study. Similarly, there is a qualitative difference between Jewish agricultural law applicable in the Land of Israel – Sabbatical years, tithing, etc. – as a series of largely ceremonial obstacles that need to be circumvented, steamrolled, or dumped in somebody else's backyard, and those same laws adapted to modern circumstances in a Jewish state in a way that honors their purpose and intent. There are many more elements of Jewish tradition that take on new meaning when they are observed by an entire society and not just a select minority.[2]

I can't venture a guess as to the specifics of how all this will play out. As Itcha Meir's kids and Bentzi's kids and Adi's kids find more common ground in their diverse paths toward some authentic form of national Judaism, we will no doubt witness a process of fermentation. Remember, I'm not talking about the likes of Americans like Heidi or Ben bending Jewish observance to reconcile it with a dominant outside culture that they have internalized or aspire to internalize, but rather Jews in a Jewish state seeking to live Jewish lives. This much I know: as Israelis from diverse backgrounds begin to speak the language of halakha more fluently, and as they continue to speak to each other, their halakha will become more like Shimen's – balanced across the moral flavors, less focused on signaling, fluid as the Oral Law is meant to be, and less uptight and anxious than halakha under constant threat.

Will their commitment be deep enough, their knowledge broad enough, their practices specific enough? I can't say. Will the preponderance of Israeli Jews resist the cheap attraction and universalizing effects of American pop culture sufficiently to participate in this process? I hope so, but can't offer guarantees. But

---

2. Some recent books, published in Hebrew, have tried to put their fingers on a new kind of Judaism that might be developing in Israel. See Yoav Sorek, *HaBrit HaYisraelit* [The Israeli Covenant] (Tel Aviv: Yediot, 2015); Shmuel Rosner and Camil Fuchs, *Yahadut Yisraelit* [Israeli Judaism] (Tel Aviv: Dvir, 2018); Micah Goodman, *Ḥazara Beli Teshuva* [Return without Repentance] (Tel Aviv: Yediot, 2019). See also Evelyn Gordon and Hadassah Levy, "Halacha's Moment of Truth," *Azure* 43 (2011), which specifically considers a number of the issues raised in these paragraphs.

I am willing to venture that a version of halakha that will emerge from the collective efforts of those who do participate will, in some crucial ways, assume qualities *beyond* Shimen's; it will be more meaningful than symbolic, normal rather than defiant, and less baroque and esoteric.

This last point bears explanation. In the normal course of events, languages become more complex with the natural accretion of increasingly nuanced grammatical rules and oddities; in this sense, halakha is no exception. Moreover, when halakha is observed by a select minority and the study of Torah is left to an even more select minority, it is sometimes made deliberately opaque to keep impostors from meddling. But when languages are adopted by many non-native speakers or when speakers of different dialects are suddenly thrown together, an opposite process takes place and the language's grammar is simplified;[3] this already happened with the transition of biblical Hebrew to the simpler, modern Hebrew we now speak. It is likely that a similar process will take place with halakha: as many come closer to tradition and as the integration of communities from different diasporas accelerates, we will see a greater focus on principles common to diverse Jewish communities at the expense of marginalia specific to particular communities or to aficionados of esoterica.

FREEDOM

The ferment of which I speak has been made possible by the ingathering of exiles in a Jewish state. It took several generations, but the freedom and purpose that Israel has provided the Jews is finally resulting in a generation of young people who not only have a sense of mission and responsibility, a strong desire for self-sufficiency, and confidence in themselves and in each other, but

---

3. John McWhorter, *Language Interrupted: Signs of Non-Native Acquisition in Standard Language Grammars* (New York: Oxford University Press, 2007).

also a realistic assessment of what is achievable and what is utopian and a thirst for authentic Judaism that can serve as a foundation for personal, communal, and national life. In short, Israel's success is the precise *opposite* of what many of its founders saw as its purpose. Instead of overcoming Jewish tradition, it has facilitated a return to it; instead of replacing Jewish communities with the state, it has given such communities the space and the confidence to flourish and to cross-pollinate.[4]

To complete this process, Israel needs to provide its citizens freedom not only from foreign enemies and foreign cultures, but from their own government and from unelected power-brokers. Education in Israel would be better and more balanced if bureaucrats would let schools choose curricula and parents choose schools; communities would be more connected to religion if bureaucrats let communities appoint (or not appoint) rabbis and run their own religious services; we'd all be more equal if the state didn't empower academic and judicial elites that enforce their own self-serving versions of equality. The continued excessive power of Jewishly acculturated elites like Adi has driven us to the edge of a cultural abyss; it is the healthy instincts of the traditional majority that will rescue us.

The old Zionist notion that the big state will guide its citizens to the ideal balance of Jewishness and democracy has it exactly backwards; it is the limited "night watchman" state that seeks to do no more than keep us safe – or, more precisely, that serves as the framework within which we keep each other safe – that will

---

4. In this context, it is worth mentioning, in particular, Jews who immigrated to Israel from Islamic countries in the early days of the state and whose traditionalism was in some ways similar to that of Shimen. (A discussion of the traditionalism of these communities is beyond the scope of this work.) This traditionalism was initially subdued by the secular Zionist establishment, then re-asserted itself somewhat aggressively through the Shas party, and now serves as one possible model for those seeking a scalable version of traditional Judaism.

create the opportunity for us to figure it all out for ourselves slowly but surely.

Some ideologues still think that we are on the verge of messianic times and it's our duty to restore the top-down control of society by a revived Sanhedrin or Politburo or Council of Sages. But they are all mistaken. The rabbis say that the messianic era will be distinguished only by freedom from political subjugation,[5] and that messianic redemption is one of those things (along with scorpion bites and windfalls) that come only when we are least expecting them.[6] The redemption of the Jewish people will not be bestowed by the state; rather, if we will it, it will be the result of slow development from the bottom up, as healthy Jewish instincts under conditions of freedom are gradually made manifest in the public sphere. If the state and all the determined do-gooders just leave us alone, one day, when we are least expecting it, we might just look around and think to ourselves: You know what, here we are, free Jews living in a Jewish country, building it and sustaining it, studying the Torah and more or less living by its commandments, raising proud and non-neurotic Jewish kids. Free at last. Free at last. Thank God Almighty, we are free at last.

* * *

Let's finish by returning to the dining hall in Princeton where this book began. I've written this book in response to Heidi's challenge to the justice of my tribal loyalties and her insistence that the appropriate lesson of the murder of six million Jews is the danger of parochialism, including Jewish parochialism. But the truth is that when that conversation actually took place, I just sat there slack-jawed, staring at her uncomprehendingly.

---

5. Shabbat 63a.
6. Sanhedrin 97a.

Had I been a bit less naive and sheltered, had I the vaguest idea where she was coming from and what she wanted from my life, I might have simply said the following:

I make no more apologies for my tribal loyalties than I do for my family loyalties. I'm a Jew both by blood and by choice, and my life has meaning precisely because I share with other Jews a history and a destiny, and a system of duties that connects one to the other. As for your implied assertion that tribal loyalty comes at the expense of universal love, you have it backwards. No society can function for long without leveraging the lessons of a specific developed tradition. No society will do good for others without a moral system that first inculcates kindness to kin and clan. No society will produce decent human beings without arbitrary-seeming rules that restrain base animal instincts. No society will have the will to bear children, to invest love and energy in them, and to teach them good from bad, without believing that it has some mission on this earth that gives life meaning and purpose.

I don't doubt that your advocacy of universal love comes from a genuine longing to make the world a better place, but I'm equally convinced that high-sounding enlightened platitudes won't get you any closer to that goal. You'll only cut yourself off from your own people and your own best hope to be part of a project that will give your life direction, while most of your carefully curated collection of ethnically diverse friends will have the good sense to combine the skills they've learned in university with allegiance to their own cultures and traditions.

I might have gone on in this vein, making all the arguments I have marshaled in this book, telling Heidi all about Shimen. Heidi would no doubt have challenged me with strong counter-arguments and pointed out important issues that I elided. Are the claims I've made about Jewish tradition unique to Judaism or could other religions make similar claims? To what extent are cultures like Shimen's dependent on the proximity of other cultures like Heidi's to help sustain them? How does someone not born into a traditional community develop the necessary allegiances and intuitions to be a full-fledged participant?

These are excellent questions, but I'll leave it to Heidi to figure out her own answers to them.

* * *

So, that's that.

We've spoken here of some grand ideas, but when all is said and done, perhaps they're just gussied-up advertisements for the importance of humility. We can choose to live like those who, given the privileges of wealth and leisure and fueled by an exaggerated sense of entitlement, set off on a foolhardy quest to reinvent civilization in the name of cosmic justice; but then our inevitable failure is likely to leave us estranged from those who preceded us and with little to pass on to those who follow us. Or we can choose to live like Shimen and others who, even when robbed of every worldly good, live purposeful lives of quiet dignity that honor the wisdom of those who came before them and bequeath that wisdom – and perhaps just a bit more – to those who come after them.

I take leave of you now, dear reader, in the hope that in my own efforts to add just a bit more, I too have not neglected to honor and to bequeath.

Maggid Books
The best of contemporary Jewish thought from
Koren Publishers Jerusalem Ltd.